CityCareerSeries.com

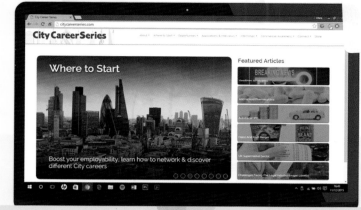

CityCareerSeries.com offers a multitude of high quality, concise and easy-to-understand tips, articles, videos and blogs:

- You will find information on boosting your employability, networking and the different types of firms and opportunities that you can apply for.
- The interactive (and syncable) calendar provides easy access to firm deadlines and links to application portals, whilst the firm profiles give you an insight into the range of City firms looking to hire graduates.
- You will find examples of application and interview questions that are typically encountered, complete with detailed suggestions of how to tackle them.
- Psychometric, situational judgement and e-tray tests are explained and techniques to help you approach them are suggested.
- Appropriate behaviour during internships is considered and hundreds of previous interns have offered an insight into their experiences whilst undertaking a variety of internships and placements at different City firms.
- Topical news stories are presented weekly, complete with explanations of why the stories may affect firms and their clients.
- Different industries have been analysed and the frameworks that can help you to conduct your own analysis of industries have been explained.
- An overview of the sources you should read to keep abreast of developments relevant to City firms and their clients has also been provided.

Social Media

 www.facebook.com/citycareerseries

 www.linkedin.com/company/city-career-series

 www.twitter.com/Career_Series

 City Career Series

Online Communities

Want to share tips and network with people at the same stage as you in the recruitment process? Join one of our online communities!

- **Commercial Law Applicants**

  www.facebook.com/groups/commerciallawapplicants

- **Commercial Law Interns**

  www.facebook.com/groups/commerciallawinterns

- **Investment Banking & Finance Applicants**

  www.facebook.com/groups/investmentbankingandfinanceapplicants

- **Investment Banking & Finance Spring Interns**

  www.facebook.com/groups/investmentbankingandfinancespringinterns

- **Investment Banking & Finance Summer Interns**

  www.facebook.com/groups/investmentbankingandfinancesummerinterns

- **Operations, Risk & Compliance Applicants**

  www.facebook.com/groups/operationsriskandcomplianceapplicants

- **Technology Applicants**

  www.facebook.com/groups/technologyapplicants

- **Consultancy Applicants**

  www.facebook.com/groups/consultancyapplicants

Contents

Introduction   **5**

What Do Investment Banks Do?   **7**
- The Role Of Investment Banks   7
- Key Departments   8

General Commercial Knowledge   **10**
- Strategic Challenges   10
- Why Acquire, Merge With Or Cooperate With A Business?   12
- How To Grow A Business   13
- How To Purchase A Business   14

General Financial Knowledge   **15**
- Introduction To Financial Accounting   15
- Financing A Deal   20
- Valuing A Business / Financial Ratios   23
- Introduction To Economics   27

Investment Banking Division   **32**
- Mergers & Acquisitions Team   32
- M&A Deal: The Process   33
- Equity Capital Markets Team   35
- Initial Public Offering: The Process   35
- Debt Capital Markets Team   37

Markets   **38**
- The Teams: Sales, Trading & Research   38
- Fixed Income, Currencies & Commodities (FICC)   40
- Cash Equities   42
- Pitching A Stock   43
- Derivatives   43

Market Sizing & Brainteasers   **46**
- Market Sizing Example Answer   48
- Brainteaser Example Answer   49
- Assumptions   50

Key Microsoft Excel Formulas & Shortcuts   **52**
- Navigation & Editing   52
- Formatting   53
- Formulas   54

General Interview & Internship Preparation   **59**
- Writing Applications & Preparing For Interviews   59
- Converting Internships Into Full-time Jobs   62

Further Reading   **66**

Introduction

This handbook offers a solid grounding in the general knowledge required for Investment Banking Division, Markets, Finance, Operations, Risk and Compliance interviews and internships. It includes: a description of the role of different banking divisions; an overview of key business, finance, economics and accounting concepts; an introduction to mergers and acquisitions, debt finance and equity finance; important banking terminology; useful Microsoft Excel formulas; general interview advice relating to competency, commercial awareness and case study interviews; and much more. This handbook is aimed primarily at students preparing for interviews and internships. For candidates who have not yet reached these stages, the Application, Interview & Internship Handbook provides guidance relating to boosting your employability, researching firms and careers, networking, structuring CVs and cover letters, answering application and interview questions, approaching psychometric tests, conducting yourself during internships and enhancing your commercial awareness.

How Should The Information In This Handbook Be Applied?

Many interviews involve firms providing candidates with case studies, business scenarios or articles. As part of the assessment, you may have to give a short presentation (these typically focus on business issues and/or how the firm can assist its clients), before then being questioned at length on various issues/discussion points. You may be questioned on topics such as: business performance, financing deals, mergers & acquisitions, investment options and the role of the firm/different departments. You may be provided with information on the background of a business; business accounts from recent years; press clippings about a business; information about a business' internal operations; and information on external developments relating to the industry in which the business operates.

Develop your understanding of business, finance and economics concepts so that you can demonstrate and apply strong commercial logic during case studies and commercial awareness interviews. If a client is considering purchasing another company, what are the different financing options and the corresponding advantages and disadvantages of each (see the *Financing A Deal* section)? How can such a transaction be structured (see the *How To Purchase A Business* section)? How else can the firm help (see the *What Do Investment Banks Do?* section)? Demonstrate an ability to flexibly apply the concepts to the facts of the case study provided and assess in that particular case study which concepts are likely to be the most relevant and effective.

How Should You Use This Handbook To Prepare?

Please take this as only a basic guide. We encourage you to research into all the terms and concepts contained within in greater depth, as they are by no means definitive or guaranteed to be wholly or objectively accurate. Terms have been defined throughout, but many of these definitions are subjective and no consensus exists as to their precise definition. We have included information which we personally found to be useful in our interviews and internships, but we researched into the terms and concepts included in greater depth and read around the subjects to ensure our understanding was sufficient to intelligently discuss the concepts with interviewers and supervisors.

We recommend that you use this handbook as a framework around which interview preparation can be structured. If you decide to discuss the concepts contained within this handbook during the interview process, you are likely to be tested on your application of them, both in fictitious case studies and in the context of real work, clients and industries. Rather than merely memorising/regurgitating the definitions and concepts contained within this handbook, ensure your understanding is strong. We were tested on many of the concepts after bringing them up in a variety of interviews and could not have succeeded had we not truly understood them.

Please do not be overwhelmed by the sheer volume of potentially brand new content contained in this handbook. We were not expected to know all of this information in any one interview; the concepts contained within were merely of use at some point throughout the 30+ interviews that we collectively attended. However, understanding the concepts contained within this handbook could give you an essential edge and is more important and valuable than simply recalling technical terms. Discussing them in the context of interview case studies, or with supervisors when they set you related work during internships, can lead to positive feedback in relation to your commercial awareness/interest.

Which Opportunities Can You Apply For?

- Investment banks tend to offer Spring Weeks for 1st year students doing a 3-year degree and 2nd year students doing a 4-year degree. Spring Weeks typically include work-shadowing opportunities, group exercises and presentations from investment bankers and graduate recruiters, but typically involve little or no responsibility. These opportunities may (depending on the bank) also lead to fast-track opportunities and at the very least, they provide evidence of your research and commitment to the career. This can therefore bolster your application for a summer internship later on.

- Full 10-12 week summer internships are then typically available for penultimate and final year students, although some internships on offer also cater to graduates. These internships typically involve candidates in real work (which can mean much longer working hours!) and candidates may also have to undertake a range of assessments throughout.

We have produced a series of videos and articles that give you an insight into the recruitment process for investment banks and the range of opportunities that are available. These can be viewed at:

www.CityCareerSeries.com → Where To Start? → Introduction to Investment Banking

The interactive (and downloadable) calendar on our website provides easy access to a multitude of firm deadlines and links to application portals. This can be found at:

www.CityCareerSeries.com → City Firms & Deadlines → Calendar

We have put together a selection of firm profiles that give you an insight into the range of investment banks that offer insight experiences, internships and graduate roles. These can be found at:

www.CityCareerSeries.com → City Firms & Deadlines → Investment Banking

Acknowledgments

A huge thank you to Yash Zaveri, Lauren Cooper and Claire Leslie (Warwick Law School Careers Consultant) for their extensive and invaluable edits. A huge thanks to the City Career Series team (Carly Schogger, Nowtash Alsafar and Chris Phillips) for their incredible hard work, creativity and enthusiasm. Thanks to Donna Schogger and Frida Gundmark for all their helpful suggestions and proof reading. A massive thank you to Christopher Stoakes for all his advice and support and for providing the inspiration for the City Career Series handbooks.

Thanks to all those that have supported us throughout this project, in particular Danny Schogger, Poppy, Kai Majerus, Raj Nandwani, Hugh Beale and the lawyers and bankers that we met whilst on internships for all their lectures, inspiration, proof reading, comments and suggestions. Thank you to Vinay Mistry (vinay@vinaymistry.com) for designing citycareerseries.com and Chris Phillips (www.cphillipsdesign.uk) - who deserves a second mention - for his endless patience and fantastic graphic design work.

Thank you to the members and the executive committee of Warwick Finance Societies for all the positive responses and useful feedback relating to earlier drafts of this handbook over the years.

Please note that the firms that have contributed to this handbook are only responsible for the information contained within their particular articles.

What Do Investment Banks Do?

Investment banks are confusing organisations to understand at first, especially in light of the fact that a plethora of acronyms are used to describe everything from divisions and geographies to financial products and markets. The easiest way to familiarise yourself with the relevant jargon is to spend time inside investment banks and talk to those who spend most of their days (and many nights!) working in them. This overview is aimed at those looking to gain a basic insight into the workings of an investment bank. It should enable the reader to present him or herself with the necessary confidence and understanding of the industry to succeed during interviews and internships. Remember that the fundamental role of an investment bank is to connect organisations seeking capital (money) with investors looking to invest funds in order to grow their own capital.

Investors

- Investors seek a return on their investment that at least matches the rate of inflation. They usually invest in companies or securities if the potential return on investment exceeds the return that could be achieved via other means (such as saving in a bank account or purchasing government bonds). In this context, investors are typically high net-worth individuals, private equity firms or corporate entities referred to as investment funds. The latter includes the companies to which we pay our pension contributions (pension funds) and insurance premiums (insurance companies), mutual funds and sovereign wealth funds.

Organisations Requiring Capital

- Companies require capital to acquire other firms and assets, invest in new ventures, expand into new regions and finance operations. Governments require capital to facilitate investment or repay older debt that has fallen due.

Investment Banks

- intermediaries between investors and organisations requiring capital. The way in which the financial markets operate is often very complex, but banks are essentially the conduits of capital. Without the service of wholesale, investment or merchant banks, companies would find it far more difficult to raise capital (and thus expand and invest) and investors would struggle to access investment opportunities that could grow their capital.

📖 **Institutional Investors / Investment Funds:** institutions with specialist knowledge that trade (buy and sell) securities (such as shares, bonds or derivatives) in large quantities, usually on behalf of others. Examples include: asset managers, mutual funds, hedge funds, pension funds and insurance companies.

📖 **Pension Funds & Insurance Companies:** pension funds invest the pension contributions made by employees/employers in order to generate a return that will enable them to provide retirement income for employees when they reach the end of their working lives. Insurance companies invest insurance premiums in order to make a profit and to ensure enough capital is generated to cover insurance claims in the future.

📖 **Hedge Funds:** these are sophisticated investment firms that aim to generate high returns from investments using advanced investment strategies. These firms typically have short-term investment horizons and invest capital that has been borrowed from investment banks. Hedge funds try to make money regardless of whether the market moves up or down.

📖 **Private Equity Firms:** these aggregate funds from institutional investors and private individuals. They aim to purchase mature businesses with established strategies and reliable cash flows, at low prices, using large quantities of debt. Through improving operational efficiency (e.g. cutting costs) and using financial engineering techniques (e.g. paying down (paying off) debt using operating cash flows), private equity firms aim to increase the value of companies in which they have invested. Typically, they look to then sell on the companies for a profit after 3-5 years of ownership and improvements.

📖 **Venture Capital Firms:** these also aggregate funds from institutional investors and private individuals. They invest in companies at a very early stage (sometimes before companies have generated any profit) and often use industry experts to help grow the business.

📖 **Sovereign Wealth Funds:** state-owned investment funds that invest for the benefit of a country's economy and citizens.

📖 **Securities:** financing or investment instruments such as bonds and shares.

📖 **Cost Of Capital:** the cost for an organisation to raise and sustain capital. For capital sourced through borrowing (debt capital), this is the cost of the interest payments a borrower must make to a lender. For equity investments (e.g. share purchases), this is the reward demanded by investors to compensate for the risks relating to their equity investment. Potential rewards include capital gains (which occur when shares are sold for more than they were purchased) and dividend payments. Potential risks include the fact that share prices may fall and that there is no legal obligation for companies to pay dividends to shareholders. The cost of capital can vary depending on current market conditions and an organisation's financial performance, maturity and creditworthiness (including its track record and the nature of any previous relationships with investors). Organisations will usually be willing to pay a reasonable price for capital, based upon the assumption that they will be able to generate financial returns (from investing that capital) that exceed the amount paid to investors for their capital (the cost of capital).

📖 **Premium:** paying a premium means paying an amount that exceeds the market value of a product or company. Premiums can be offered by potential purchasers (or borrowers) to persuade sellers (or lenders) to engage in transactions. Buyers will offer premiums in the belief that they will be able to extract additional value from the target company post-acquisition, either because it is under-valued, underperforming or unable to operate as efficiently as it could if controlled by the buyer.

Key Departments

The term 'investment bank' may be slightly misleading at times, as not everyone who works at an investment bank is strictly an investment banker. However, the below summary should help to clarify the roles of various departments within investment banks. More detail on some of the teams and departments mentioned is included later on in this handbook.

Investment Banking Division (IBD)

This division's fundamental role is to advise corporates, governments, high net-worth individuals (or families) and other institutions on corporate finance matters, most notably mergers and acquisitions (M&A) and raising finance. This includes work involving the equity capital markets (ECM) and debt capital markets (DCM). The Investment Banking Division may also offer services such as liability management, risk hedging, derivatives advice and restructuring. Bankers work together with companies to assess their options and then implement their chosen courses of action.

📖 **Capital Markets:** these are financial markets that link organisations looking to raise capital (through selling equity and/or debt instruments) with investors looking to supply capital (through buying equity and/or debt instruments). Products including shares, bonds and securitised products are traded between governments, companies, banks, private investors and other investors such as hedge funds and pension funds.

Markets / Sales, Trading & Research / Securities

The Markets Division of an investment bank is typically split up into three separate departments: Sales, Trading and Research. These each have their own individual roles, but also work together to help clients achieve their investment objectives. As with any other front office role within an investment bank, the main objective of each role is to help to generate financial gains for clients and the bank. The Sales team essentially generates trade ideas and provides market information for clients, based upon its own research and research conducted by the Research teams. Traders then execute trade requests made by (or on behalf of) clients.

Investment Management / Asset Management

Investment/Asset Management departments manage and invest in securities (such as shares or bonds) and assets (such as real estate) on behalf of clients. These clients are typically large, institutional investors such as pension funds and insurance companies.

Private Banking / Wealth Management

Private Banking (or Wealth Management) focuses more on providing services such as investment advice, efficient tax planning and financial planning. Typically, advice is individually tailored to help satisfy the unique personal and professional financial objectives of high net-worth individuals or families.

Finance

The Finance team in a bank manages the bank's internal finances. This includes reporting trades executed by the Markets teams into financial accounts; preparing the bank's management accounts and financial statements; analysing the bank's financial performance; and conducting internal auditing (which involves liaising with external auditors). Those working in Finance teams are usually expected to take accounting qualifications.

Operations

The Operations Division provides general support to the revenue generating (or 'front office') departments, helping to run and streamline a bank's internal processes. Examples of the work conducted by Operations employees include controlling and managing the processing of trades made by other divisions of the bank and trying to ensure traders receive confirmations of trades earlier and quicker than anyone else in the market (thereby ensuring a commercial advantage).

Compliance / Legal

Work that banks undertake is often governed by substantive and complex regulation and legislation. One of the core functions of the Compliance/Legal departments is to ensure that a bank complies with this regulation and legislation within the jurisdictions in which the bank operates. This can involve liaising with regulators; ensuring sufficient controls are in place to reduce the risk of non-compliance; keeping employees up-to-date on their legal obligations; and providing legal advice (whilst at times working alongside external legal counsel). Candidates should have a good basic knowledge of relevant regulations when applying for this role.

General Commercial Knowledge

Starting, running or growing a business can require the acquisition and utilisation of a wide range of resources and capabilities and typically involves a huge degree of risk. Consequently, the reality is that many new businesses fail.

Strategic Challenges

Barriers to entry may reduce the chances of a business successfully starting up or entering a new market. Such barriers include: financial barriers; complicated or restrictive regulation (for instance certain jurisdictions may not allow foreign businesses to enter particular local markets); an inability to compete against established competitors; various risks and uncertainties; and a lack of resources.

Costs

- The primary aim of most businesses is to generate profit. To do this, a business' revenue (turnover) must exceed its fixed costs and variable costs. Profits increase as costs decrease or revenue increases. Therefore, keeping costs as low as possible is essential if a business is to maximise its profit margins.

📖 **Profit Margin:** the amount of profit generated per item after deducting the average cost of producing each item.

📖 **Revenue / Turnover / Sales:** the total income generated from a firm's operations within a period of time. This does not take into account costs, instead purely reflecting the money that has been received from consumer sales. For example, if a company sells 10 handbooks for £8 each, its revenue would be £80.

📖 **Fixed Costs:** business costs that remain the same regardless of the number of units produced or sold. Examples include: the rent paid for an office or a factory; the cost of paying utility bills; or the cost of fuel for an aeroplane flight. These costs will all remain the same (or almost the same) regardless of whether a company sells 0 or 1000 units.

📖 **Variable Costs:** costs that change in relation to the number of units produced or sold, for instance the cost of packaging or delivering each individual product. Labour to some extent is a variable cost as over time, the number of employees may change to reflect a company's level of output. However, in the short term, labour is generally a fixed cost.

- There are various strategies that businesses can employ to minimise or stabilise costs. For instance: maximising economies of scale; integrating into the supply chain; outsourcing; offshoring; entering long-term contracts; and utilising derivatives.

📖 **Economies Of Scale:** the cost advantage gained as output increases. This cost advantage arises when fixed costs are spread across a greater quantity of sales. When organisations place larger orders with suppliers, suppliers will usually pass on a proportion of the cost savings they receive through economies of scale to that firm, in turn reducing that firm's input costs.

📖 **Integrate Into The Supply Chain:** the supply chain is comprised of contributors involved in the process leading up to the sale of a product (e.g. manufacturers). Typically, each contributor will charge prices that include a profit margin. If one company takes control of two or more stages in the supply chain, it will not have to pay this additional margin and costs will consequently decrease.

📖 **Outsourcing:** contracting out various roles or processes to external companies, for instance customer services, distribution, or marketing. Businesses can benefit in numerous ways, for example through outsourcing to parties with greater expertise or experience in undertaking a particular role; or through the flexibility outsourcing may enable. For instance, if demand for a firm's products or services decreases, it must still pay employee wages (at least in the short term). However, if a firm outsources its labour requirements (i.e. pays another company to provide employees as and when they are required) and demand subsequently decreases, the firm can simply end its contract with the company that provided the employees. This would enable the firm to consequently avoid paying for employees that are no longer needed (subject to the terms of the outsourcing agreement).

📖 **Offshoring:** shifting elements of production or distribution abroad, usually to countries in which costs (e.g. labour) are lower.

📖 **Long-Term Contracts:** these can enable companies to more accurately predict future costs, or to mitigate the risk of price increases if, for instance, the price of raw materials increases globally. Participants in the supply chain may also provide more favourable rates to businesses willing to commit to long-term relationships.

📖 **Derivatives:** financial contracts relating to underlying assets (such as securities or commodities). Examples include futures, which are agreements between parties to engage in a transaction on a predetermined future date at a specified price; and options, which give one party the right (but do not obligate them) to purchase or sell a product on a predetermined future date at a specified price. These derivatives can help companies to better predict future costs and mitigate the risk of adverse price movements reducing profitability (this is known as hedging risk). This can in turn facilitate more accurate financial planning.

To learn about the Profitability Framework and how to apply it in case study interviews, check out:

www.CityCareerSeries.com → Applications & Interviews → Case Study Interviews

Competition / Saturated Market

- If there are existing competitors in the market that are more established it may be difficult for new businesses to compete. Established businesses may benefit from having recognisable brands and trusted relationships with consumers. The consequent customer loyalty may prevent customers from switching to a product offered by a new market entrant.

- Established businesses are also more likely to receive preferential rates from supply chain participants such as suppliers, reducing costs to a level that new businesses would struggle to match (having had little or no opportunity to earn good will or trust). In addition, an established business may benefit from economies of scale, enabling superior cost control and wider profit margins than that which a new entrant may be able to attain. Consequently, established firms may be able to undercut prices charged by new entrants.

- To compete in saturated markets (markets with many competitors), new firms may thus require a unique selling point. Firms could offer a product or service with unique attributes that differentiate that product from those sold by competitors, or find a way to significantly undercut competitor prices (as Ryanair did in the airline industry). Such unique selling points could provide new entrants with a competitive advantage, resulting in a greater chance of success.

Uncertainty

- If businesses produce new products, uncertainties arise as to whether there will be sufficient demand for those products to generate profit. Conducting extensive market research before fully investing in the design, production, distribution and marketing of products can mitigate this risk, enabling businesses to modify and adapt offerings to suit consumer preferences.

Resources / Capabilities

- Does the company have human resources with the necessary capabilities (skills, experience and expertise) to create, brand, distribute and market a viable product or service? Does the business have the necessary physical resources to successfully operate, most notably start-up capital, cash for operations, machinery and offices?

- A business lacking the necessary capabilities and resources could consider partnering with other businesses or employing people who have: relevant business experience, a network of beneficial contacts (which could facilitate the financing, production and distribution processes), knowledge of the target market, or the resources required to effectively operate. For example, small businesses could share resources such as office space, whilst start-ups could partner with individual investors willing to provide capital and other relevant resources in exchange for equity. Such investors are typically known as business angels.

Why Acquire, Merge With Or Cooperate With A Business?

Businesses acquire, merge with or cooperate with other businesses for a variety of reasons, many of which relate to the synergies that can arise. However, a less permanent solution may be to engage in alliances, partnerships or joint ventures, which give rise to similar benefits but also enable parties to retain some autonomy.

📖 **Acquisition:** when one business purchases another, either through mutual consent or through a hostile takeover.

📖 **Merger:** when multiple businesses voluntarily and permanently combine to form one business.

📖 **Alliance / Partnership:** when businesses or individuals with complementary capabilities/resources cooperate in order to advance their mutual interests. For example, the inventor of a product may engage in a partnership with a lawyer, distributor or marketing agency. The parties typically share the costs, risks and rewards.

📖 **Joint Venture:** when two or more businesses agree to pool their resources and work together on a specific task or project, such as the development or launch of a product. The parties typically share the costs, risks and rewards.

📖 **Synergies:** synergies refer to the benefits that can result from the interaction between two companies. Examples of synergies include: the sharing of resources to reduce costs and the sharing of knowledge/human resources to improve product offerings. Synergies can ensure that the value generated by companies that have been combined exceeds the overall value that those companies could produce separately.

Below are some of the advantages of acquiring/merging with/cooperating with other companies:

✓ **Access To New Markets And Customers:** this should facilitate an increase in sales.

✓ **Access To Complementary Resources:** organisations can boost their own capabilities. For instance other businesses or partners may possess physical, financial or technical resources, expertise (market specific knowledge), complementary skills, supply chain relationships (for instance access to suppliers and distributors), or networks and contacts that enable firms to circumvent barriers to entry and compete more effectively.

✓ **Economies Of Scope:** firms may benefit from collaborations that will enable them to diversify their product range. Selling a greater range of products could attract new customers and consequently increase sales. Bundling products with those of complementary businesses (for instance a mobile phone manufacturer linking with an Internet service provider or mobile game creator) could also improve a businesses' product offering.

✓ **Efficiency:** if organisations combine and enlarge their operations, this could enable them to buy, produce and sell in greater quantities, consequently giving rise to increased economies of scale and thus lower costs. Integrating into the supply chain (by acquiring or partnering with supply chain actors) could reduce external costs. In addition, combining knowledge, expertise and resources could enable firms to increase operational efficiency and thus reduce internal costs.

✓ **Savings:** companies could share costs such as infrastructure rent, marketing or research and development.

✓ **Reputation:** organisations may influence others' perceptions of their capabilities through gaining external legitimacy, which can in turn increase trust from suppliers, lenders and customers. Linking with an established organisation in a new market (for instance Tesco partnering with Tata in India) may reduce consumer suspicion, encouraging consumers to make purchases.

✓ **Innovation:** increasing access to resources and capabilities may foster innovation.

✓ **Competition:** forming alliances with, merging with, or acquiring other businesses reduces direct competition in the market. This can increase a firm's market power, which lessens its need to reduce prices in order to compete.

There are however issues that can arise when businesses combine/cooperate:

✗ **Loss Of Control / Conflict:** profits and decisions may have to be shared. Reaching an efficient consensus on decisions may be difficult if the motives or objectives of the parties involved do not align.

✗ **Administration / Costs:** coordinating and integrating different businesses can be a complex and costly process.

✗ **Inefficiency:** communication issues may arise if an organisation becomes more complex. In addition, multiple alliances with similar partners may yield fewer benefits than partnerships with differentiated partners.

✗ **Expropriation:** a larger, more powerful company may steal customers, expertise, assets or processes and then terminate the agreement. Ensuring intellectual property rights are sufficiently protected can mitigate this risk.

How To Grow A Business

Businesses can achieve growth organically; through acquiring or merging with other businesses; through expanding into other markets (e.g. countries); or through engaging in an alliance with one or more other businesses.

Organic Growth

Growth facilitated by an increase in demand achieved, for instance, through effective marketing and branding, expanding distribution (perhaps through exporting), diversifying the product range, licensing or franchising. Below are some of the advantages and disadvantages of growing a business organically.

- ✓ **Reduced Risk:** there is generally less risk in the sense that growth depends more on a natural increase in demand, rather than estimates and projections of the potential returns that an acquisition could generate.

- ✓ **Easier Integration:** easier for a firm to retain its culture, protect its brand and maintain effective communication.

- ✗ **Slow Expansion:** growth may be slower than growth achieved through acquiring other organisations.

- ✗ **Costs:** it can be expensive to build brands from scratch in new jurisdictions, as this can require extensive market research and large-scale promotional campaigns.

- ✗ **Increased Risk:** Foreign Direct Investment (FDI), for instance opening a new store abroad, is risky as it can be difficult to break into new markets if more established competitors exist. In contrast, exporting or franchising can be less risky alternatives, as these do not require direct investment (such as purchasing a factory or an office building abroad).

> 📖 **Exporting:** when firms sell products from their home country to other countries. It can enable firms to expand their operations without committing to direct investment in another country, thus reducing risk and costs. However, distribution (e.g. transportation) costs, currency value fluctuations and potentially high taxes may hinder effective cost control.

> 📖 **Franchising:** when firms sell the right for others to set up identical firms under the same name (using the same brand and selling the same products) in exchange for a lump sum payment and/or royalties. This can enable rapid expansion that boosts a franchisor's brand exposure and customer base. A franchisor can usually exert some control over a franchisee to ensure that the franchisee does not act in a manner that damages the brand. Starbucks and Burger King are good examples of franchises.

> 📖 **Licensing:** when one firm permits another firm to use an element of its business, for instance the right to manufacture its products, incorporate its technology into a product or use its intellectual property (IP) rights, usually in exchange for a royalty. If a firm lacks the capabilities to commercialise a product but has developed the technology, licensing to a firm that can commercialise it could provide a source of revenue. However, if the technology is embedded into a product, the licensor may generate little brand recognition or customer loyalty. There is also a risk that the licensee will expropriate the technology and emerge as a competitor.

Acquisitive / Equity-Based Growth

Growth achieved through acquiring, merging with or working with other companies. This can involve sharing profits and risk. Below are some of the advantages and disadvantages of acquisitive/equity-based growth.

- ✓ **Rapid Expansion:** can facilitate rapid expansion through providing immediate access to, for instance, distribution networks, customers, employees, or retail outlets that are under the control of another firm.

- ✓ **Additional Experience:** one firm can benefit from the experience that another firm may have accumulated in new markets. This can help it to learn about new markets quickly, reducing the costs associated with market research and increasing its chances of commercial success.

- ✗ **Costs:** it can be very costly to purchase other firms, as payment of a premium for the target company's shares (payment of a higher price than the market value) and extensive fees to legal/financial advisors may be required.

- ✗ **Time:** it can be very time consuming to purchase other firms, as ample negotiation and shareholder consent may be required.

- ✗ **Complexity:** effective integration can be difficult to achieve if the organisations involved are large and complex.

How To Purchase A Business (Structuring A Transaction)

When deciding how to purchase a business, buyers must consider whether a share or an asset purchase best suits their needs. Below are some of the advantages and disadvantages of different methods of purchasing a business.

📖 **Share Sale/Purchase:** this involves a purchaser buying either all of another company's shares, or a controlling stake in another company.

✓ **Control:** easier for purchasers to gain full control over a company, including its human capital, tangible assets (e.g. plant and machinery) and intangible assets (e.g. business relationships, good will/brand loyalty, intellectual property rights, and knowledge of internal processes).

✓ **Savings:** purchasers are exempt from goods and services tax if acquiring assets through a share sale.

✗ **Shareholders:** it may be difficult for purchasers to persuade a sufficient proportion of shareholders to agree to a sale.

✗ **Risk:** purchasers will take on sellers' existing liabilities and obligations.

📖 **Asset Sale/Purchase:** this involves a purchaser buying specific assets owned by another company, such as buildings or patents.

✓ **Flexibility:** the flexibility to acquire only the assets that compliment a purchaser's existing business can result in a transaction that is more financially efficient.

✓ **Valuation:** valuation may be less subjective as intangible assets such as customer loyalty need not be considered.

✓ **Due Diligence:** due diligence relating to specific assets may be quicker and easier to conduct than firm-wide investigations.

✓ **Risk:** it is less risky in the sense that a purchaser has a lower risk of taking on unforeseen liabilities.

✓ **Tax:** tax law in the UK enables the market value of assets purchased to be offset against tax, even if the purchaser paid less than the market value.

✗ **Control:** purchasers will not gain full control over the entire company and may thus fail to benefit from any employees or internal knowledge and processes that may have helped to facilitate efficient and effective utilisation of the assets.

📖 **Due Diligence:** refers to the process under which a potential buyer and its advisors carry out in-depth investigations into many aspects of a proposed target company, in order to gain a solid understanding of that company's business and/or market. Due diligence can help a potential buyer to decide whether to go ahead with the purchase and if so, at what price and on which terms.

We have produced some additional resources to help you structure your analysis of problems in case study interviews. These can be found at:

www.CityCareerSeries.com → Applications & Interviews → Case Study Interviews

General Financial Knowledge

Introduction To Financial Accounting

In order to understand the process of valuing a company, it is necessary to have a solid understanding of financial accounting and the key financial statements that comprise financial returns. In the UK, all registered companies are required to file financial accounts. However, publicly listed companies and private companies with a turnover exceeding £6.5 million are required to produce and publish more substantial, fully audited financial accounts. For investors, financial accounts may indicate the viability of different investment options. They provide an insight into a company's financial performance and financial standing. For investment bankers, financial accounts are the building blocks for an analysis of a company's ability to create shareholder value (returns for shareholders in the form of capital appreciation and/or dividends) and meet interest repayments (for example, payments to banks that have lent the company money). There are three key financial statements that candidates should understand:

1. **The Income Statement**: this measures a company's revenue, expenses (including interest and taxes) and after-tax profit over a year; and

2. **The Balance Sheet** (or Statement of Financial Position): this provides a snapshot of a company's financial position at a particular date (usually the end of the year).

3. **The Cash Flow Statement**: this measures a company's cash inflow and outflow over a year.

Income Statement

The Income Statement (known historically in the UK as the Profit and Loss Account) details a company's financial performance resulting from its day-to-day operations over a defined period of time (typically one year). It shows the income generated from a firm's operations over a period of time; the expenses relating to those operations; and the net profit (also known as the 'bottom line' as it appears at the bottom of the Income Statement). Different companies may report their Income Statements in slightly different ways. The below example provides a simplified illustration of an Income Statement, including an outline of the key elements.

Income Statement	
Revenue / Turnover / Sales	**£ XX.XX**
– Cost of Goods Sold (COGS)	£ (XX.XX)
= Gross Profit	**£ XX.XX**
– Selling, General & Administrative Costs (SG&A)	£ (XX.XX)
= Earnings Before Interest, Tax, Depreciation & Amortisation (EBITDA)	**£ XX.XX**
– Depreciation & Amortisation	£ (XX.XX)
= Operating Profit / Earnings Before Interest & Tax (EBIT)	**£ XX.XX**
– Interest Payments	£ (XX.XX)
= Profit Before Tax (PBT)	**£ XX.XX**
– Tax	£ (XX.XX)
= Net Profit	**£ XX.XX**

📖 **Net Profit:** refers to the amount of money remaining from the revenue after all related expenses have been subtracted.

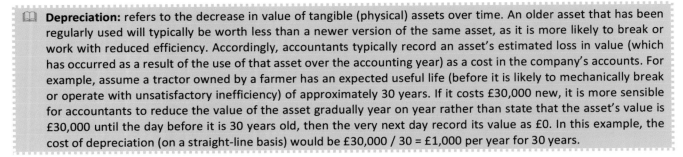

📖 **Cost Of Goods Sold (COGS):** includes the direct costs associated with each sale made (usually variable costs). For example, if a firm sells 1,000 desks, such costs would include the direct costs associated with manufacturing each desk (e.g. the wood used).

📖 **Selling, General & Administrative Costs (SG&A):** includes general expenses that do not directly relate to each individual sale (usually fixed costs). Examples include overheads such as office rental payments and utility bills and purchases of assets.

Certain costs may be difficult to neatly categorise within COGS or SG&A. For example, the cost of labour may not directly correlate with the number of sales that are made. Wages (at least in the short-term) will still have to be paid even if demand (and consequently output) decreases. However, a reduction in sales (and output) could eventually lead to redundancies, indicating that labour costs may to some extent correlate with the number of sales made in the long-term. In recognition of this, certain costs can be categorised (within reason) at the discretion of the person creating the accounts.

Depreciation and amortisation account for the depletion in value of company assets over time. Depreciation and amortisation are not technically cash expenses; they should be thought of more as economic expenses associated with the running of a business. Depreciation applies to tangible assets, whereas amortisation applies to intangible assets (such as patents owned by pharmaceutical companies or software used by technology companies, which will eventually become out-dated).

📖 **Depreciation:** refers to the decrease in value of tangible (physical) assets over time. An older asset that has been regularly used will typically be worth less than a newer version of the same asset, as it is more likely to break or work with reduced efficiency. Accordingly, accountants typically record an asset's estimated loss in value (which has occurred as a result of the use of that asset over the accounting year) as a cost in the company's accounts. For example, assume a tractor owned by a farmer has an expected useful life (before it is likely to mechanically break or operate with unsatisfactory inefficiency) of approximately 30 years. If it costs £30,000 new, it is more sensible for accountants to reduce the value of the asset gradually year on year rather than state that the asset's value is £30,000 until the day before it is 30 years old, then the very next day record its value as £0. In this example, the cost of depreciation (on a straight-line basis) would be £30,000 / 30 = £1,000 per year for 30 years.

📖 **Amortisation:** refers to the decrease in value of intangible assets over time. For example, a patent may decrease in value as its expiry date approaches. Accordingly, accountants typically spread the decrease in value of intangible assets (as a cost on the Income Statement), for accounting purposes, over the duration of the asset's useful life.

It should be noted that interest payments are deducted from the revenue before tax is calculated. Accordingly, the larger the interest payments a company must make, the smaller its tax bill becomes (tax is calculated based on earnings left over after interest payments have been deducted). The Income Statement is often followed by a separate statement of shareholders earnings, which details dividend payouts made from the net profit.

In case studies, you may be presented with basic financial accounts from the current year and the previous few years. If this is the case (depending on the issues you are asked to consider), start by analysing the profit figures to see how the company's performance has changed.

- If profits have increased year on year, this could indicate that the company could continue to thrive. Conversely, if the net profit has decreased, this could, on the face of it, suggest it may eventually run into financial difficulties. At this stage you should then try to discover (through looking at the accounts) *why* the net profit has decreased.

- For instance, a decrease in revenue (which could cause a corresponding decrease in net profit) could suggest consumers are purchasing less of the company's products, which in turn may indicate that new competitors have entered the market (or that existing competitors have developed a similar or superior product, perhaps at a more favourable price).

- If the revenue has remained the same or increased but the net profit has decreased, look at whether the costs have increased (which would also decrease the net profit). If costs have increased, does this suggest the company has failed to implement effective mechanisms to control costs (in which case think of potential solutions, for instance laying off staff or looking for cheaper suppliers?) or has the cost of raw materials increased (e.g. if the company produces apple juice, has the price of apples increased)? Alternatively, has the company made an investment (for instance purchased a factory) that has increased costs in the current year (and thus reduced the net profit) but may well contribute to an increase in net profit in future years?

Cash Flow Statement

The Cash Flow Statement is perhaps best explained by way of an example. Supermarkets buy goods from a large number of suppliers on credit. This means that the suppliers allow the supermarkets to take possession of the goods for a certain period of time (e.g. 30 days) before they must actually pay. Supermarkets then generally sell the goods on to customers in the interim period. Those customers typically pay immediately. Under such circumstances, accounts payable (the amount still owed to suppliers for goods already supplied under the credit agreement) is greater than accounts receivable (the amount owed to the supermarket by its customers). The fact that the supermarket effectively hoards cash received from customers for a certain period of time before paying back the suppliers means it is operationally cash positive (assuming the items received are sold).

One way of measuring the extent to which this applies to a business is through calculating its 'working capital'.

Working Capital	=	Current Assets	–	Current Liabilities
		(including accounts receivable)		(including accounts payable)

Having a low (or negative) working capital figure can mean that the company lacks sufficient current assets to pay its current liabilities, suggesting it may to some extent be financially unstable. Note that if the company is genuinely unable to pay its debts, then it may well have to cease trading. If the working capital figure is too high however, this may suggest that the company is failing to invest its excess cash, which is financially inefficient. The optimal working capital figure often depends on the particular company and industry.

The Cash Flow Statement shows the actual movement of cash in and out of a company over a period of time (typically 1 year). It is important to understand the fundamental difference between profit and cash. The profit figure contained within the Income Statement (which is determined by revenue and costs) is based upon the number of legally concluded transactions, regardless of whether any cash has yet been transferred (for instance if goods have been supplied on credit). However, the Cash Flow Statement shows the actual transfer of cash in and out of a company during a given time period and will detail the previous year-end cash balance and end with the new cash balance.

Cash Flow Statement	
Cash Flow From Operating Activities Including revenue received from sales, payment of wages and other costs such as interest payments and tax expenses.	**£ XX.XX**
Cash Flow From Investing Activities Including capital expenditure on machinery, intangible assets or the cost of acquisitions etc.	**£ XX.XX**
Cash Flow From Financing Activities Including inflows of cash received as a result of corporate financing activities (for instance money received as payment for issued shares or bonds); and outflows of cash relating to these inflows (for instance interest or dividend payments).	**£ XX.XX**
Increase (Or Decrease) In Cash	**£ XX.XX**
Cash At Start Of Period	**£XX.XX**
Cash At End Of Period	**£XX.XX**

Balance Sheet / Statement Of Financial Position

The Balance Sheet (BS), also known as the Statement of Financial Position (SOFP), provides a snapshot of a company's financial situation. It lists the value of everything a business owns (its assets) and everything the business owes (its liabilities). The equation underpinning the Balance Sheet is:

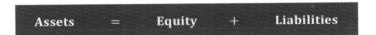

| Assets | = | Equity | + | Liabilities |

All financial events in the life of a company must be accounted for through the recording of two corresponding entries in the Balance Sheet. Company assets (which form one side of the Balance Sheet) must have been supported through the use of some sort of financing (detailed on the other side of the Balance Sheet), either in the form of capital (equity) or through the company taking on debt (liabilities).

> 📖 **Asset:** something of value to a company. Tangible assets include machinery and factories. Intangible assets include intellectual property rights, customer loyalty and knowledge. On a Balance Sheet, it is generally the tangible assets that are accounted for.

For example, if a company raises £1 million through selling shares and takes out a loan of £1 million when it first incorporates (starts up and registers as a company), its total assets will amount to £2 million.

- This £2 million will be recorded as:

    (a) £2 million cash in the 'Current Assets' section of the Balance Sheet; and

    (b) £1 million in the 'Equity' (share capital) section and £1 million in the 'Liabilities' section on the other side of the Balance Sheet.

- If the company subsequently purchases a building for £500,000, then cash (on the 'Assets' side) will reduce to £1.5 million and a new category will be created (also on the 'Assets' side), typically called Plant, Property & Equipment, the value of which will be £500,000.

- In the meantime, the Equity and Liabilities side of the Balance Sheet will remain unchanged as no new share capital has been received and no new debt has been taken on.

- If £500,000 of the loan is then paid off using cash, the 'Assets' section will decrease by £500,000 (to reflect the fact that cash has been spent on paying off the debt) and there would be a corresponding decrease in the 'Liabilities' section (to reflect the fact that the value of the outstanding loan has reduced to £500,000).

The Balance Sheet is essential in investment banking for the financial analysis of a company, as it contains information on the company's capital structure. There is a typical example of a Balance Sheet on the next page.

> 📖 **Capital Structure:** this refers to the proportion of a company's capital (financial resources) that is attributable to debt and the proportion of the company's capital that is attributable to equity. This in turn can affect a company's ability to raise additional capital or its attractiveness to investors. For instance, a company that is highly in debt will be perceived as a riskier investment by potential lenders or investors.

Balance Sheet / Statement Of Financial Position

Assets

Current Assets £ XX.XX

Including cash, receivables (payments due from customers), inventory and other assets that will either be sold or removed from the Balance Sheet within a year.

Non-Current Assets £ XX.XX

Including machinery, buildings, long-term investments (including stakes in other companies) and other assets that will remain on the Balance Sheet for longer than a year.

Total Assets **£ XX.XX**

Equity

Retained Earnings £ XX.XX

Net profit minus dividends

Share Capital £ XX.XX

Capital received from issuing shares

Liabilities

Current Liabilities £ XX.XX

Including short-term debt, payables (money owed to suppliers etc.), tax liabilities and other liabilities that will be removed from the Balance Sheet within a year.

Non-Current Liabilities £ XX.XX

Long-term debt and equivalents (e.g. pension liabilities) and other liabilities that will remain on the Balance Sheet for longer than a year.

Total Liabilities + Equity **£ XX.XX**

Financing A Deal

In its early stages, a business may take out small loans, apply for government grants, or receive investment from venture capital firms/business angels. As a business grows and matures, it may use its cash resources to fund day-to-day operations and increasingly use debt (where the investors are lenders) or issuances of equity (where the investors become part-owners). Large businesses may combine multiple forms of financing, for instance issuing shares (equity) whilst also taking on multiple layers of debt from different sources (for instance taking loans or issuing bonds). Note that businesses may borrow money even if they have cash available. For instance, a business may choose to invest available cash in a new venture and borrow money to fund day-to-day operations (or use available cash to fund day-to-day operations and use money borrowed to invest in a new venture) in the hope that the profits generated by that new venture will exceed the cost of borrowing money to use in place of the available cash.

If a business becomes insolvent, the ways in which the repayment of different creditors is organised and prioritised can depend on the type of financing they have provided (debt or equity) and the nature of the contractual agreements made between the parties. The repayment of senior debt holders is prioritised over the repayment of other creditors if a company becomes insolvent. They generally receive lower interest payments, as they are more likely to be repaid and often take security over a company's assets. Junior (subordinated) debt holders are ranked below senior debt holders and therefore will only be repaid once senior creditors have been repaid in full (if any money remains). Subordinated creditors may charge more interest to compensate for this additional risk.

📖 **Cash Reserves:** financing operations using existing cash resources (for instance, retained profit).

✓ **Control:** the owners retain full ownership and control of the business and its assets.

✓ **Cost Savings:** no interest payments or dividends will need to be paid.

✓ **Arranging Finance:** businesses can access their own capital immediately and without incurring hefty administration fees.

✗ **Effectiveness:** some firms may not have enough cash to finance investment and maintain sufficient cash flow.

📖 **Bank Loan / Overdraft:** firms can borrow from banks and then pay back the loans in instalments, plus interest. The interest rate can be fixed (making it easier for a business to predict its costs) or floating, in which case the rate may be linked to the fluctuation of a benchmark interest rate (for instance LIBOR), which could in turn end up costing less than fixed rate repayments if interest rates happen to fall or, contrary to expectations, remain static. A bank may be persuaded to issue a loan on the strength of a well-prepared business plan, a strong previous relationship with the borrower, a financial guarantee from another party, or a company's ability to provide collateral.

📖 **Syndicated Loan:** where multiple banks (the 'syndicate') work together to contribute funds in order to provide the required capital. The banks share interest payments from the borrower and risk. Syndicated loans are more viable where borrowers require a large amount of capital, as these loans can be complicated and expensive to administer.

✓ **Control:** the owners generally retain full ownership and control of the business so long as repayments are met. Note however that lenders may be able to exert some control over a borrower's business through taking security over assets on terms that restrict the ability of the borrower to sell those assets.

✓ **Cost Savings:** money can be borrowed as and when it is required, meaning that the borrower may only have to make interest payments that reflect the actual capital in use (i.e. the money drawn out of the bank account). In addition, interest payments made are tax deductible.

✓ **Effectiveness:** banks are generally more suited to complicated lending structures as they have extensive experience of evaluating risk. They may thus be more inclined to approve financing and once a loan is approved, a business is generally guaranteed to receive the full amount immediately. Banks may however decide to hedge risk through releasing funds in instalments. This could prevent borrowers from using capital recklessly or for purposes not previously agreed. Under such circumstances, borrowers may only qualify for new instalments once certain targets have been met.

✓ **Arranging Finance:** small loans are quicker and cheaper to arrange than bond or share issues. However, as mentioned, large, syndicated loans may be incredibly costly and complicated to arrange.

✗ **Security:** collateral may be required in return for a loan, typically in the form of an asset. If repayments are not met, lenders may seize and sell any secured assets in order to retrieve their money. In addition, companies lacking valuable assets may struggle to secure loans due to their inability to offer sufficient collateral.

✗ **Costs:** interest payments may be substantial, depending on a borrower's credit rating and the economy.

✗ **Repayable On Demand:** certain loans (notably overdrafts) are repayable on demand, which could cause cash-flow issues if repayment is demanded earlier than expected.

📖 **Bond Issue:** this is where a company (the 'issuer') sells bonds (similar to IOUs) through the debt capital markets. Bonds are purchased by investors and entitle them to a periodic interest payment (coupon) in addition to a lump sum repayment of the principal amount after a set period (when the bond 'matures').

✓ **Control:** bond issuers do not have to offer bond purchasers security over their assets (meaning issuers remain free to use their assets as they see fit) and bondholders rarely try to restrict a bond issuer's business operations.

✓ **Effectiveness:** access to multiple investors through the capital markets makes it easier to raise large amounts.

✗ **Demand:** if a company has a low credit rating or a low profile, it may struggle to sell enough bonds to raise all the capital it requires (and banks may be unwilling to underwrite the issue). To stimulate demand, companies sometimes offer bonds with higher returns (known as 'high yield' or 'junk' bonds).

✗ **Arranging Finance:** bond issues are expensive to arrange, as many terms need to be set out. A bond issue is therefore unsuitable for companies raising only a small amount of capital.

📖 **Underwriters:** bond issues involve underwriters (investment banks) which typically agree (for a fee) to purchase all the bonds in advance and then sell them on to investors, or to purchase any unsold bonds post-issuance.

📖 **Prospectus:** legally required document that must precede bond or share issues. It advertises the issue to potential investors and contains information about the issuer's business, the potential risks and the issuing firm's financial circumstances in addition to the terms and conditions of the issue.

📖 **Share Issue:** this is where a company sells ('issues') its shares. Investors provide money in exchange for shares that represent an ownership stake in a company, with the aim of reaping returns in the form of capital growth (if those shares are later sold at a profit) and dividends (if the company elects to pay dividends).

📖 **Initial Public Offering (IPO):** this is where a company lists its shares on a stock exchange for the *first* time (hence the phrase *initial* public offering) in order to sell those shares through the equity capital markets. Listing through a stock exchange also facilitates the subsequent trading of those shares.

📖 **Business angels:** business angels (or "angel investors") are wealthy individuals who invest their personal income in early-stage businesses in exchange for equity. Working with a business angel can be especially beneficial for a business if that business angel has ample knowledge of, and experience working in, that business' industry.

In general, the advantages and disadvantages of equity investments can include:

✓ **Cost Savings:** no interest payments are required, thus preserving cash flow. In addition, if the company goes bankrupt, the loss is spread across all shareholders.

✓ **No Security:** no security is required, meaning a company will not risk having its assets seized as a result of it issuing shares and subsequently failing to generate sufficient profit.

✓ **Complementary Skills:** some investors (e.g. business angels and private equity firms) may contribute skills, experience, expertise and contacts that benefit the company.

✓ **Profile:** listing on a stock exchange can enhance a company's profile. This can increase its access to the market for capital and enable it to negotiate more preferential terms with suppliers and creditors.

✗ **Control:** equity represents a stake of ownership and thus control among existing owners is diluted as additional shareholders join. Shareholders are afforded certain rights including the right to vote and significant company decisions may be subject to shareholder approval. A company may also become vulnerable to a hostile takeover as it can do little to prevent existing shareholders from selling their shares to investors that are attempting to acquire a controlling stake.

✗ **Demand:** if insufficient demand exists, a company may fail to raise all the capital it requires.

✗ **Costs:** profits must usually be shared between more people, although paying dividends is typically discretionary.

✗ **Administration:** share sales can be time consuming, complicated and costly to administer and once a company is publicly listed, it is subject to continuing (and at times onerous) disclosure requirements.

📖 **Security:** taking security over a borrower's assets can increase a lender's chances of receiving back its money if the borrower defaults on the loan. There are many types of security, including mortgages, fixed and floating charges and guarantees. Security can give a lender the legal right to claim and sell the asset(s) over which it has taken security (in order to recover the funds loaned) if a loan is not repaid in accordance with the terms agreed by the parties. For example, a mortgage over a house (which is a form of security) typically entitles the lender to sell the house and recover money it is owed if the borrower fails to meet its repayment obligations.

There are other factors that a company must consider when choosing between different methods of financing, including: its level of existing debt; the assets it has available to grant security over; any restrictions on its flexibility to borrow; its particular objectives; and current market conditions. These factors can affect the 'cost of borrowing', i.e. the size of the interest payments it will have to make to compensate a lender for the risk of giving the loan. Lenders may be unwilling to lend to riskier borrowers, or may only be willing to lend if those borrowers are willing to make high interest payments (lenders may feel that the risk is worth the potential for a high financial return).

Assets

- The extent to which a borrower has valuable assets over which security can be taken can determine whether (and if so, on which terms) a lender will be willing to lend.

Capital Structure

- The amount of debt a company has already taken on may affect the viability of different methods of financing.
- If a company has a high ratio of debt in comparison to equity, this means it is 'highly geared' and indicates it may lack sufficient assets to support debt repayments if additional debt is taken on. Lenders may therefore perceive highly geared companies as more risky borrowers and consequently charge them higher interest rates (or even refuse to lend them capital).

The Market

- **Demand:** if the value of a company is low, or it lacks a high profile or strong reputation, it may be unable to sell a sufficient number of shares or bonds at a price high enough to raise the required level of capital.
- **Market Conditions:** during an economic downturn, businesses in general perform less well (in part due to a decrease in consumer spending). This can reduce the willingness of investors to lend money at viable interest rates or invest in shares due to the increased risk of businesses becoming insolvent or underperforming.
- **Interest Rates:** interest rates are typically higher for borrowers with lower credit ratings. This is because lenders may demand a higher premium to compensate them for the increased risk of such borrowers defaulting. Therefore, debt financing may be less viable for companies with low credit ratings due to the potentially high cost of borrowing.
- **Banks:** issuing bonds may not be viable if investment banks are unwilling to underwrite the issue (which may be the case for firms with low credit ratings). In addition, banks may refuse to lend to firms lacking assets that can be used as collateral.

📖 **Credit Rating Agencies:** these assess the likelihood of organisations or sovereigns being able to repay their debts. If a company has a high credit rating, its debt is perceived as a less risky investment and the company can typically borrow at a lower interest rate as a consequence. The main agencies that rate the credit of organisations and sovereigns are Moody's, Standard and Poor's and Fitch.

Restrictions / Flexibility

- A company's existing debt agreements and/or Articles of Association may prohibit it from taking on further debt.
- Existing shareholders may not approve a new share issue (a rights issue), especially if the company's earnings-per-share figure suggests that not enough profit is being generated to provide sufficient returns to all shareholders if additional shareholders are introduced. The company's Articles of Association may also place some restriction upon share issues.
- If businesses wish to remain flexible, issuing shares or bonds may be preferable as the terms upon which loans can be obtained from banks may be more restrictive. This is not always the case however, depending on the terms of a bond or share issue.

📖 **Articles Of Association:** a document drawn up by the founders of a company at the time it is incorporated. It defines the duties, obligations, rights, powers and limitations of the company, directors, shareholders and other members.

📖 **Rights Issue:** where existing shareholders receive the option to purchase additional shares, usually at a discount, in proportion to their existing shareholding. This option enables companies to raise new capital whilst affording existing shareholders the opportunity to retain the proportion of ownership that they had held before the new share issue.

Time Frame

- If a business requires short-term funding or immediate access to capital, taking a loan or using cash reserves may be preferable to issuing equity or bonds, which in contrast is generally a long-term commitment and can take a long time to set-up.

Valuing A Business / Financial Ratios

One of the fundamental services investment banks offer to clients is to provide a valuation of their business (usually in the context of an M&A transaction or when the company raises equity). A simple analogy for understanding how a business is valued is that of how one might consider a house to be valued.

There are two broad methods by which the value of a house may be determined. The first is a market-based method, which could involve comparing the value of properties with similar characteristics (such as size and location) or the price paid for similar properties in the past. The second is an intrinsic valuation method, for example valuing a house based on its ability to generate rental income.

In the context of valuing a business, the same principles apply. A market-based valuation of a public listed company could involve an investor taking into account the price paid for other similar businesses in the market. An intrinsic valuation would focus more on the cash flows that the company has generated (or could potentially generate), based upon the company's financials.

Enterprise Value

The term enterprise value is typically used to refer to the total price someone would have to pay to acquire a business (i.e. to purchase all the equity in the business and as a result, assume all of its debt liabilities). A buyer might choose to pay off debt immediately post-acquisition or to pay it off later. In other words, enterprise value refers to the true cost of owning the business.

$$\text{Enterprise Value} = \text{Equity Value} + \text{Net Debt}$$

📖 **Equity Value:** this essentially refers to the market capitalisation of a business.

📖 **Net Debt:** this is a metric that measures a firm's ability to repay its debts if they were all immediately due. Cash and cash equivalents that sit on a company's Balance Sheet are subtracted from the total debt to give the 'net debt' as these items could theoretically be used to immediately pay off some of the debt. Net debt will be a negative number that contributes to a reduction in the enterprise value figure.

The above formula is a simplified illustration of the calculation of a company's enterprise value. Although this will often suffice for the purpose of an interview, it is useful to note that a number of additional items are often added and subtracted to this simplified formula in order to yield a more precise definition of 'enterprise value'.

Discounted Cash Flow (DCF)

DCF analysis can also be used to estimate a company's enterprise value. It can assess the intrinsic value of a company, based solely upon its financial information. The figure is 'discounted' or 'adjusted' to take into account the changing value of money over time. The sum of all future cash flows (in and out) is known as the net present value (NPV) and this can help to determine whether a proposed investment is financially viable. Calculating DCF can be incredibly complicated and as such, we recommend that you study textbooks to gain a strong understanding of how this method of valuation works. For IBD internships in particular, strong knowledge of this calculation method is frequently expected. Note that if the company is not listed on a stock exchange, there are other calculations that must be made (however this is beyond the scope of this handbook). To calculate DCF, you can use the following steps:

1. Calculate the free cash flow to the firm (FCFF) for X number of years

FCFF must be estimated for each separate year into the future (typically 5-7 years into the future) based upon various assumptions (e.g. industry trends and assumptions of growth).

$$\text{FCFF} = \text{EBIT} - \text{Tax} - \text{Capital Expenditure} + \text{Depreciation \& Amortisation Costs} - \text{Change In Net Working Capital}$$

2. Calculate the weighted average cost of capital (WACC)

The WACC is the amount of money the company must pay on average to raise and sustain capital.

$$WACC = [\text{Cost of Debt} \times (1 - \text{Tax Rate}) \times \frac{\text{Debt}}{\text{Debt + Equity}}] + [\text{Cost of Equity} \times \frac{\text{Equity}}{\text{Debt + Equity}}]$$

📖 **Cost Of Debt:** the cost of debt will be calculated using the average interest rate paid by the company (per year) on its outstanding debt (e.g. bonds or loans).

📖 **Cost Of Equity:** the cost of equity is calculated using the **Capital Asset Pricing Model (CAPM)**, illustrated below:

| Cost of Equity | = | Risk Free Rate | + | Equity Risk Premium | x | Company's Beta |

📖 **Risk Free Rate:** the figure often used is the 10 or 30-year US Treasury Bill (government bond) yield.

📖 **Equity Risk Premium:** the average return of the stock market (on which the company is traded) in excess of the risk free rate, over a significant period of history (e.g. the last 10 years, but usually much longer than this).

📖 **Company's Beta:** a measurement of how closely movements in a company's share price tend to correlate with movements in the overall stock market. A beta of 1 would mean that if the stock market as a whole fluctuates (e.g. its total value increases by 10%), the company's share price should fluctuate in exactly the same way (e.g. rising by 10%). Assuming the stock market increases by 10%, if a company has a beta of 0.5 this would imply that the share price would likely rise by 5% (0.5 x the change in the overall value of the stock market). A beta of 1.5 would imply an increase of 15% (1.5 x the change in the overall value of the market). Low betas are typically associated with utility companies (e.g. energy companies) whilst high betas usually apply to more risky companies. Conversely, a beta of -1 would mean that if the stock market as a whole fluctuates (e.g. its total value increases by 10%), the company's share would move in the opposite direction by the same amount (e.g. decreasing by 10%). A beta of -1.5 would imply a decrease of 15% and so on.

3. Discount the expected FCFF for future years

Once each separate FCFF has been calculated, they must each be discounted, using the WACC.

$$\text{Discounted FCFF Year X} = \frac{\text{Estimated FCFF Year X}}{(1 + \text{WACC})^X}$$

X = the number of years into the future in which the particular cash flow being estimated is expected to be.

As X increases, so does the number by which the estimated FCFF is divided, which in turn reduces its (present) value. As such, the further into the future that we project each FFCF, the lower the value of each projected FFCF present value becomes. These estimations are discounted in this way to take into account the time-value of money, inflation (which reduces the purchasing power of each unit of currency) and the likelihood of receiving the cash flows.

📖 **Time Value Of Money:** the 'time value of money' is based upon the premise that a set amount of money in the present is worth more than the same amount of money will be in the future due to its earning capacity in the interim period. Take the following example as an illustration of this concept. A set amount of money today, for instance £100, is worth more than that £100 would be in the future. This is partially due to the fact that the £100 could be invested (for instance in return for interest payments or capital gains) in a manner that leaves the investor with, for example, £150 further down the line.

4. Calculate the terminal value

The terminal value of the company must next be calculated. This aims to account for the cash flows that will be received in the years beyond those already forecasted (i.e. the first 5-7 years into the future), which are too far into the future to accurately estimate. The terminal value is calculated as follows:

$$\text{Terminal Value} = \frac{\text{Final Year FCFF x } (1 + g)}{\text{WACC} - g}$$

g = the perpetual growth rate (typically the estimated growth rate of a country's economy in the long- term).

5. Discount the terminal value

This terminal value must be discounted similarly to the other forecasted cash flows to arrive at its present value.

$$\text{Discounted Terminal Value} = \frac{\text{Terminal Value}}{(1 + \text{WACC})^X}$$

6. Add together all the discounted FFCFs and the terminal value

The sum of all the discounted FFCFs must then be added to the discounted terminal value of the company to give the intrinsic enterprise value of the firm. This example illustrates the required calculation where FCFFs have been estimated for 7 years into the future (the '…' signifies that the values for years 3-6 would also have to be projected, discounted and added together).

$$\text{DCF} = \frac{\text{FCFF Year 1}}{(1 + \text{WACC})^1} + \frac{\text{FCFF Year 2}}{(1 + \text{WACC})^2} + \cdots + \frac{\text{Final Year FCFF (Year 7)}}{(1 + \text{WACC})^7} + \frac{\text{Terminal Value}}{(1 + \text{WACC})^7}$$

It must be noted that assumptions such as the perpetuity growth rate strongly impact the overall valuation and therefore this method is still fairly subjective.

Earnings Before Interest, Tax, Depreciation & Amortisation (EBITDA)

EBITDA is one of the most commonly used profit metrics in investment banking. The metric is useful because it excludes items that are subjective or unrepresentative of a firm's true ability to generate cash. No account is taken of any interest or tax payments made, or any accounting adjustments made to reflect the depreciation of assets or amortisation. These exclusions make it easier to compare two similar companies on a like-for-like, operational basis, providing investors with a better indication of which company is more inherently profitable.

- **Interest:** excluded because interest figures are affected by a firm's capital structure (the amount of equity it has issued and debt it has taken on). If Company A and Company B were exactly the same (produced the same products, incurred the same costs and sold them for the same price), but Company A had borrowed more capital than the other, the additional interest payments paid by Company A would likely result in Company B reporting greater profits (even though Company B has equal potential to generate similar profit, pending a restructuring of its capital structure). EBITDA therefore provides an indication of the profit attributable to all of the firm's capital providers combined (lenders and investors) as it stands before interest.

- **Tax**: the level of tax paid is dependant on the tax jurisdictions in which a company operates and its capital structure. Excluding tax therefore enables a better assessment (for the purpose of comparison) of companies' inherent ability to generate profit. For instance Company A may generate similar revenue to Company B and achieve equally as efficient cost management. However, Company A may report lower profit figures as a result of its tax bill. In addition, if Company B is financed primarily through debt, its tax bill may be lower as interest payments are tax deductible.

- **Depreciation & Amortisation**: excluded because these figures are fairly subjective from an accounting perspective. This is because there are different permitted methods of calculating depreciation and amortisation (for instance the straight line and reducing balance methods). The discretion afforded to accountants can therefore enable them to exercise this discretion in order to present companies in a more positive light. For this reason, it can be preferable to directly compare two firms if they are excluded.

EV/EBITDA Ratio

When valuing Company A, investors may start by looking at the enterprise value (the market value of the equity and the net debt) of a similar company, for example Company B. They will divide Company B's enterprise value by its EBITDA to calculate its EBITDA multiple; then multiply Company A's EBITDA by Company B's EBITDA multiple to estimate the enterprise value of Company A. For instance, if Company B's enterprise value is £1million and its EBITDA is £100,000, its EBITDA multiple would be 10. If Company A's EBITDA is £50,000, this would then be multiplied by 10 to give an estimated enterprise value of £500,000.

Price To Earnings (P/E) Ratio

The P/E ratio illustrates the relationship between the current market price of a company's shares and the profits that the company generates. A lower P/E ratio is an indication that the price of a company's share is lower in relation to the overall profits of the business and thus that the company may provide a better option for investment (depending on variables such as the industry average). Potentially profitable companies in their early stages may not have generated much (or any) profit, which would give rise to a low earnings per share figure. As such, the P/E ratio may be more useful for comparing or valuing more mature companies.

$$P/E \text{ Ratio} = \frac{\text{Share Price}}{\text{Earnings Per Share (EPS)}}$$

$$\text{Earnings Per Share} = \frac{\text{Net Profit}}{\text{Number Of Shares Outstanding (NOSH)}}$$

Combined Value

An investor could consider the additional value a target company could bring to their existing business. Does the target business complement their existing business in a manner that could increase the overall value of the newly combined company post-combination? Could a merger help an investor to reduce costs (through enabling greater economies of scale or boosting their bargaining power with suppliers); acquire complementary skill sets and expertise; reduce competition; or increase their overall influence in the market? If so, an investor may be willing to pay a premium in order to acquire another business.

Comparable Analysis / Precedent Transactions

Investors would likely also take into account the prices that have been paid for comparable businesses (for instance businesses that are similar geographically, in size or operationally) under comparable circumstances.

Future Potential Of The Business

Investors could consider the overall prospects of the market in which a business operates and whether any opportunities are likely to arise that will boost profitability. For instance, if a sports equipment chain in London is the subject of a valuation and investors are aware that the Olympics are set to commence in the near future, they may be willing to pay a greater amount for the business in the knowledge that sales are likely to significantly increase during and after the Olympics. Growth projections for similar products, businesses and industries may also be taken into account. Investors could consider where a target business' products are at in the product life cycle. Do the products have the potential to sell at a similar rate to that which has generated current profitability levels, or will sales likely diminish? For instance, if a patent belonging to a target business is about to expire, competitors may be able to subsequently copy and sell the technology themselves, attracting customers away from the target business.

📖 **Product Life Cycle:** the period over which a product enters and eventually exits the market. The number of sales typically increases after a product is released and initially marketed. The number of sales then tends to stabilise and eventually diminish as more competitors enter the market and the product is replaced by cheaper or superior alternatives.

Intangible Resources

Consider whether the target business has formed political, social or commercial relationships that could be beneficial. Take into account the value of human capital. For instance, does the business have a unique management team that affords it a competitive advantage?

Introduction To Economics

This section is designed to give a very basic overview of some of the fundamental economics concepts that may be relevant for investment banking interviews and internships. It by no means provides a substantive account and far more reading, research and study is required to gain a solid grounding in the subject. Microeconomics may be of greater use when engaging in case studies, whereas macroeconomics may be of greater use when discussing current affairs.

Microeconomics: Supply & Demand

Microeconomics studies the interaction between buyers (consumers) and sellers (firms) and the factors that influence their decisions. It can provide an insight into the ways in which setting different prices for products will affect the quantity of products demanded (purchased) by consumers, which in turn can help sellers to determine the optimal price they should charge for products and the quantity of products that they should produce at that price to achieve maximum profitability.

📖 **Supply:** the quantity of a product or service available for consumers to purchase at a specific price.

📖 **Demand:** the quantity of a product or service that consumers are able and willing to purchase at a specific price.

If demand for a product increases to a greater extent than the supply of that product, firms may be able to charge a higher price for it. This is especially the case if there is an excess of consumers competing to purchase the product at a particular price.

- In such instances, whilst a price rise would inevitably deter some consumers from purchasing the product, the excess demand that had existed at the lower price indicates strong demand should still exist at a slightly higher price.

- However, if prices are increased too dramatically, demand may fall to a level that generates less profit overall than would have been generated at the original price.

Accordingly, for a company to generate optimal profit levels, a balancing act must be struck between generating as much profit as possible per individual sale and generating as many sales as possible. In contrast, if supply increases to a greater extent than demand, firms may have to reduce prices to increase demand (and thus ensure a greater number of products are sold overall). There are numerous elements that can affect supply and demand:

1. Price / Output

- Analysis of supply and demand trends can inform business decisions relating to the price at which products should be sold to consumers and the quantity of goods that should be produced by firms (firm output) at each potential selling price. This is because such analysis can provide an insight into the ways in which consumer demand (the quantity of sales made) will fluctuate at different price levels.

- Naturally, as prices increase, demand will usually fall, as fewer consumers will be able or willing to purchase the goods in question. For instance, a supermarket may sell 1000 apples in a day if they charge 30p per apple, but if the price charged were to rise to £1, the number of sales would likely decrease significantly. However, the way in which price affects demand varies depending on the type of product being sold.

📖 **Price Elasticity Of Demand:** measures the extent to which price changes affect demand. Price-elastic products are products for which demand changes significantly in response to price changes. Examples include necessities (every-day household items) or generic items that can easily be purchased from other suppliers. Price-inelastic products are products for which demand changes less dramatically in response to price changes. Examples include luxury goods such as designer items, which are less easily substituted by other products.

2. Competing Goods

- Demand may be affected by the price of identical or similar goods. For instance, if Supermarket A sells their own brand of baked beans for 50p and subsequently Supermarket B reduces the price of its own brand of baked beans to 30p, demand will likely fall for Supermarket A's baked beans and increase for Supermarket B's.

3. Substitute / Complementary Goods

📖 **Substitute Goods:** products that a consumer could purchase to satisfy the same purpose, need or want as a different product sold by another company. For instance, a train ticket may be a substitute for a plane ticket (if the route is similar) and if the price of rail travel drops, consumers may consequently decide to take a train rather than fly where possible.

📖 **Complementary Goods:** products that can or must be purchased alongside another product. For instance, petrol is a complementary product to cars. If the price of petrol dramatically increases, consumers may (in the long term) be less inclined to purchase cars.

- Demand may also be affected by the price and availability of substitute goods or complementary goods. For instance, a fall in the price of a substitute product may increase the demand for that product and consequently reduce the demand for goods to which the substitute product serves a similar purpose. In contrast, a fall in the price of a complementary good may increase demand for products to which it is a complement, as the cost of the overall package will reduce.

4. Input Costs / Profit Margins

- The quantity of goods supplied may also depend on the input costs involved in producing the goods. If costs are low and the potential profits are high for a product, supply will likely increase as it is more beneficial for firms to produce and sell this product (existing firms may increase output and other firms may enter the market). If supply increases, firms may end up having to consequently compete on price in order to generate additional sales, resulting in the price decreasing for consumers.

Macroeconomics

Macroeconomics studies changes and trends in the economy as a whole at regional, national and international levels. It examines economy-wide phenomena such as changes in unemployment, interest rates, Gross Domestic Product, economic growth and inflation. A macroeconomic change in one area will typically have knock-on effects in other areas.

📖 **Bank Base Interest Rate:** the interest rate at which national central banks lend money to domestic banks.

📖 **Inflation:** the rate at which the prices of goods and services rise. When an economy experiences inflation, each unit of currency buys fewer goods and services. Inflation is the primary reason products cost more today than decades ago.

📖 **Aggregate Demand:** the overall amount of goods and services demanded within a particular economy in a given period.

📖 **Aggregate Supply:** the overall amount of goods and services produced within a particular economy in a given period.

📖 **Quantitative Easing:** monetary policy used to stimulate economies. It involves central banks introducing new money into the economy by purchasing financial assets in the market. Flooding the market with additional capital in such a way leaves investors with additional funds, encouraging them to increase their engagement in investment activities.

Below is a simplified illustration of how central banks can influence GDP and inflation. We recommend that you research these concepts in greater detail.

Central Bank Base Interest Rate ↓
The central bank (e.g. the Bank of England) may lower its interest rate to achieve a particular economic policy goal.

Commercial Bank Interest Rates ↓
Commercial banks (e.g. Barclays) react to changes in the base interest rate by altering their savings and loan rates.

Spending ↑
Lower interest rates encourage consumers to spend more and save less because the return on their savings is lower.

Investment ↑
Lower interest rates reduce borrowing costs, making it cheaper for firms to finance investment into new ventures.

Demand for Goods & Services ↑
If spending and investment increase, this means more goods and services are being purchased (demanded).

Employment & Production ↑
When demand increases, firms generally respond by hiring more workers and producing more goods and services to meet this increase.

Gross Domestic Product (GDP) ↑
GDP refers to the total value of all the goods and services produced within a country during a given time period, which will thus rise.

Inflation ↑
When demand for goods and services increases more than the supply, prices will increase and each unit of currency will buy fewer goods and services. The rate at which prices increase is called inflation. Inflation is the primary reason goods cost more today than decades ago.

Exchange Rate ↓
Lowering domestic interest rates encourages investors to transfer their capital to countries offering higher interest rates (in search of a greater return on investment). To do this, investors sell the domestic currency and purchase the currency of the new country in which they wish to invest. When demand for the domestic currency decreases, the currency becomes less valuable and thus its exchange rate falls.

Exports ↑
Exports increase, as a weaker exchange rate means domestic goods become more affordable for those purchasing with foreign currencies.

The Knock-On Effect Of Macroeconomic Change

📖 **Hawkish Signals:** refers to the announcement of statistics (such as a greater than expected increase in GDP or inflation) that signal to investors that the central bank is likely to increase interest rates in response.

📖 **Dovish Signals:** refers to the announcement of statistics (such as a greater than expected decrease in GDP, or deflation) that signal to investors that the central bank is likely to decrease interest rates in response.

Here are some examples of the ways in which investors may react to certain statistics or events. However, these are only examples and do not provide an objective indication of the ways in which all investors will react. For instance, some investment strategies may involve betting against the market, whilst the occurrence of certain events or changes in the economy may not necessary give rise to analogous investor interpretations or responses under different circumstances.

GDP is lower than expected

- This suggests the economy is weaker than predicted. Investors may therefore anticipate interest rate cuts in order to boost the economy.

Unemployment is much higher than expected

- This suggests overall demand for products and services (consumer spending) has fallen and as a result, less people are being employed to produce products and services.

- Investors may therefore anticipate interest rate cuts in order to stimulate spending and thus increase employment.

Inflation is much higher than expected

- This means prices may have increased by a greater amount than expected. This could be undesirable if it diminishes the value of the domestic currency by too great an extent (as each unit of the domestic currency will have less purchasing power).

- Investors may therefore anticipate an increase in interest rates in order to decrease spending (demand) and consequently stabilise inflation (or even trigger deflation).

An earthquake strikes a region

- Companies may be negatively affected by a large natural disaster. This is because, for instance, some businesses and consumers will have to spend their income on repairing or replacing assets, or may simply choose to spend less due to the uncertainty underpinning their region. In addition, transport links and other infrastructure (such as power lines) may well have been disrupted, which could hinder commercial activity.

- Investors may therefore feel less certain about the future of the region and may also expect the region's central bank to cut interest rates in order to encourage spending and investment. Consequently, investors may sell their investments in the region in order to reinvest in less risky markets and markets offering higher interest rates.

- All these factors could cause the region's home currency to depreciate. This is because once investors have sold their domestic investments, they will need to sell the currency that they received for the sale of these investments in order to buy the foreign currency required to make investments in other countries. This would increase the supply (and thus decrease the price) of the domestic currency.

A hurricane hits a major oil-producing region

- Investor concern could arise as to whether any damage caused by the hurricane would disrupt oil production and thus cause a shortfall in the supply of oil.

- Such a shortfall would likely result in oil prices increasing, which could reduce profits for companies dependent on oil.

Equity Capital Markets Team

Equity Capital Markets (ECM) teams advise clients looking to issue equity in the form of initial public offerings (IPOs) and rights issues (follow-on or secondary issues). For an IPO, the ECM (and/or M&A team) works closely with colleagues from the Equities Trading and Sales desks (on the markets side of the investment bank). Investment banks can help companies to pitch themselves to potential investors at a 'roadshow'; help to structure the issue (including advising on the optimal amount of equity that should be sold); price the shares; underwrite an issue; and perhaps assist the client in the aftermarket, for instance through pursuing a 'Greenshoe' or 'over-allotment' option.

📖 **Initial Public Offering (IPO):** this is where a company lists on a stock exchange for the first time and sells shares to investors through the equity capital markets. Investors provide money in exchange for shares representing an ownership stake in the business. They then reap returns in the form of capital returns (if shares are sold at a profit) and dividends (if the company elects to pay dividends). Share prices are linked to a firm's market value and thus fluctuate according to company performance and investor speculation. Shares are typically listed on a stock exchange to facilitate trading, thus ensuring there exists a (potentially) liquid market for the shares after the offering.

📖 **Greenshoe Option / Over-allotment Option:** a provision that may be incorporated into an Underwriting Agreement that affords the underwriter the option to sell a greater number of shares to investors than had originally been planned (in case demand exceeds expectations once the issue is made).

Initial Public Offering: The Process

The IPO market in London is currently booming. IPOs provide some of the most interesting work for investment banks, which may take the role of underwriters, coordinators or advisers.

1. Attracting The Client

The Pitchbook

- Banks must first pitch to clients in order to be selected as their advisor (or one of their advisors) for a particular transaction. This first involves banks pitching their ideas to prospective clients. Pitchbooks form part of a bank's pitch to senior decision makers of companies and contain information including an overview of the investment bank (including experience, capabilities and accolades relating to research, corporate finance, sales and trading) and the ways in which the team can add value to M&A transactions. Deal-specific pitchbooks are tailored to specific transactions (such as IPOs or acquisitions).

- Banks work on a relationship basis with corporate C-level (CEO, CFO etc.) executives and will often approach businesses with ideas for M&A transactions or corporate finance transactions (although businesses also sometimes approach banks with their own ideas). Bankers must use their knowledge and understanding of a market to convince a business of the viability of an idea in order to be mandated as an advisor or underwriter (and thus get paid). IPO pitchbooks often contain a projected valuation of the business and an insight into the equity market, for instance an estimation of the level of demand likely to arise for a new equity issue from the business.

The Presentation

- Companies may then invite banks to present their pitches at a 'beauty parade'. Although many of the factors discussed in the investment banks' pitchbooks are considered, the final decision is typically based upon a range of factors including: the relationship (prior or formed throughout the pitching process) between the prospective client and the investment bank; the reputation of the investment bank and its experience handling previous advisory mandates on similar transactions; and the bank's estimation of the amount of capital it believes it can help the prospective client to secure. Banks will often look to provide debt finance for M&A deals in parallel to providing advisory services. Both services can provide significant revenue for banks and as such, banks may offer one service for a cheaper price in order to secure an invitation to pitch, then whilst pitching attempt to generate additional business (and thus additional profit) by cross-selling other services.

The Result

- The client will typically select one or two banks as lead underwriters (or lead bookrunners), in addition to other banks to form the underwriting group (or syndicate).

2. Building The Team

Underwriters

- Underwriters are the investment banks responsible for sourcing investors. Underwriters assume liability for a deal, agreeing (for a fee) to:

  (1) Purchase all the shares in advance and subsequently attempt to sell them on to investors (temporarily taking the company's equity onto its own Balance Sheet); or

  (2) Purchase any unsold shares post-issuance; or

  (3) If the parties enter into a 'best-efforts' contract, use their best endeavours to sell all issued shares, whilst taking on no obligation to purchase any that remain after the sale.

- The number of underwriters will vary with the size of the deal. More banks are often necessary if a larger quantity of equity is to be sold, as additional underwriters will likely provide access to a greater number of potential investors. The lead bookrunners (underwriters) are often known as 'lead-left bookrunners', as their names are written on the left hand side of the deal prospectus front cover.

- The underwriters' sales forces assist the financial advisor(s) in determining an offering price for the shares. Contracts and fee structures are arranged, often including 'performance fees' for banks that are dependent on the final price of the offer.

Lawyers

- Lawyers will take an integral role in the drafting of the prospectus, ensuring that it is compliant with the extensive regulation by which prospectuses are governed (regulation may govern, for instance, the content and the structure of prospectuses) and that it accurately encapsulates the commercial decisions made by the client and its financial advisors.

Accountants

- Help to create or verify companies' financial statements and analyse the financial state of a company for the purposes of valuation and risk analysis.

3. Conducting Due Diligence

Due diligence refers to the process by which the client's advisors carry out in-depth investigations into many aspects of the client's business in order to ensure the prospectus contains information that is accurate and well informed. This in turn ensures investors are able to gain a solid understanding of the company in which they are considering investing. Once due diligence has been completed, bankers and lawyers work on the prospectus.

4. Drafting The Prospectus

The prospectus advertises the issue to potential investors and contains the facts and forecasts investors require to make informed investment decisions. This includes information about the issuer's business (such as how the company operates; how its management plans to take it forward; and how the company is expected to perform over the next few quarters), in addition to any potential risks of which investors should be aware and the terms and conditions of the issue.

5. Marketing The IPO

Once a deal is filed with the appropriate authorities, the details of the upcoming IPO are made public. In the UK, the deal must be cleared by the Financial Conduct Authority (FCA). In the US, the deal must be cleared by the Securities Exchange Commission (SEC). Copies of the prospectus are printed and then the roadshow begins.

6. Investors

Using the prospectus (in addition to other supporting documents), Sales teams from the investment banks enlisted to manage the deal contact the institutional investors with which they have relationships and schedule roadshow meetings. Members of the bank's investment banking division will typically escort the CEO of the client's business as they travel across the country (or globe) meeting prospective investors. The process of accumulating potential orders is known as 'bookbuilding'.

7. Pricing The Shares

A price range (for instance 200-220p per share) is presented to investors by the underwriting team before the roadshow begins, providing investors with an insight into the estimated value of the company. If subsequent investor demand at this price range is strong, offerings will price at the top of or even above the range. Conversely, the price will drop below the range if demand is low. The final price is decided once the underwriters are ready to formally open the order book to investors. Underwriters decide how to split the available securities between investors, using knowledge of their likely trading habits (e.g. hedge funds tend to hold securities for short periods of time). The underwriter's job is to price the shares at an optimal level that ensures the client receives as much capital as possible, whilst ensuring the offering remains attractive to investors.

Debt Capital Markets Team

Debt Capital Markets (DCM) teams advise companies looking to raise debt in a variety of forms in the debt capital markets. Sometimes debt advisory teams may also advise on raising bank debt. Recently, the US market (and increasingly the European market) has moved away from bank debt finance to public debt finance, in the form of bonds. This is primarily a result of lenders becoming subject to more onerous capital requirements (imposed through reforms implemented in the wake of the financial crisis, notably Basel III), which can make it more difficult to profitably lend large amounts of capital to companies.

> 📖 **Capital Requirements:** regulation requires banks to retain a certain amount of high-quality liquid assets on their Balance Sheets (such as cash and highly-rated government bonds). Research into the Basel III regulations to see examples of the types of capital requirements imposed upon banks.

DCM teams help companies to: market themselves (through helping to produce a prospectus with other financial and legal advisers); acquire a credit rating (or multiple ratings) from the main credit rating agencies; and then price their debt at an optimal level for both the companies and prospective investors.

Debt advisory teams tend to specialise in different levels of debt risk, from companies rated as 'investment grade' (companies with a high credit rating that are issuing debt perceived as low risk, implying that the likelihood of repayment for investors is very high) to 'junk' or 'high yield' debt (debt from companies with a lower credit rating, implying that there is a higher risk of them defaulting on debt repayments).

Restructuring teams are generally concerned with debt that has become so risky that there is little chance of the creditors being repaid in full. Their role is to help the lenders and the borrowers to reach an agreement (compromise) whereby the borrower has a chance of avoiding insolvency and the lenders have a chance of retrieving at least some of their capital.

> 📖 **Insolvency:** a company is insolvent when it cannot pay its debts in time, or when the total of its liabilities exceeds its assets. If a company becomes insolvent, it must cease trading.

Markets

The fundamental role of the Markets division of an investment bank is to help clients to achieve their investment objectives. The key departments within the Markets division are the Sales, Trading and Research departments. It is worthy to note that the ways in which banks label this division vary, for instance Barclays calls this division Global Markets, whereas Citigroup calls it Sales & Trading.

Sales, Sales Trading and Trading teams will normally be split by region, sector or both depending on the bank. For example there may be a Pan European team, Emerging Markets team, Asia Pacific team and a North American team, each dealing with similar asset classes, but which relate to different regions. Teams split by regions may require individuals on the Sales or Sales Trading team to speak a particular language.

The Teams

Sales

The Sales team can be seen as the voice and face of the bank and much of its role involves personal contact with clients, traders and researchers. As such, an ability to build relationships and communicate effectively is of the upmost importance. Sales people essentially sell trade ideas to clients on the buy-side (i.e. the clients looking to purchase assets). These ideas are generated either through a Sales person's personal opinion on how the market is likely to change (based on their own research), or from work conducted by the Research department. The Sales team then facilitates the execution of trades that clients wish to pursue based upon these ideas, through acting as an intermediary between clients and the Trading teams. Sales people source information on pricing and supply from traders. They may then request traders to execute trades on behalf of clients (if clients decide to proceed).

Sales people are also typically expected to manage and nurture client relationships, which at times may involve providing clients with a general insight into what is happening in the markets. There is a constant tension that members of the Sales team must effectively balance. They must ensure their clients remain content (through securing them good prices on trades, otherwise clients could simply trade through a different bank) whilst ensuring the traders are not pushed to set prices at an inappropriate level (so that the bank can still make money).

Sales people must be strong multi-taskers as well as being able to handle pressure when booking trades and talking to clients. Sales people must also have strong attention to detail when booking trades, as wrongly recording trades could result in the desk distorting its true profit or loss figures.

It is worthy to note that, particularly in the cash equities business, the roles of Sales and Trading teams are not always clearly distinguished and some people take the role of Sales Traders, essentially combining the roles of both Sales people and Traders.

> 📖 **The Buy-Side:** the side of the financial markets comprised of investors looking to purchase assets with the aim of generating financial returns. Firms that invest, such as hedge funds and asset managers, are on the buy-side.

Trading

Traders directly participate in the financial markets through trading financial securities on behalf of clients. However, traders do not usually have direct contact with clients. Instead, they tend to deal with members of the bank's Sales team, who act as intermediaries. They aim to generate profit through taking advantage of securities' price movements in the market that occur as a result of fluctuations in supply and demand. To help predict where and when these price movements will occur, traders consider: commercial news and announcements (for instance, the imposition of new regulation); global events that could affect the supply and demand of a product (for instance an oil spill); historical price patters; and general market trends.

The role of traders is essential as they generate liquidity in the markets, meaning that they act as a channel through which investors can buy or sell their assets. Different teams usually exist to trade different assets such as equities, fixed income securities, commodities, currencies (FX) and derivatives. Traders in investment banks are known as market-makers, as they help to determine the prices at which assets can be bought or sold through influencing levels of supply and demand. Traders are required to quote their position in a market if they are asked.

Even though traders may work as a team and share similar goals, trading can be a very individualistic role as traders are measured (and to some extent remunerated) based upon their personal performance, as set out in their Profit and Loss (P&L) account. Traders are expected to make quick, informed decisions; have strong analytical skills; and be proficient at arithmetic. They must also have comprehensive knowledge of the markets in order to manage risk and generate profits.

There are a number of ways in which a trader can manage risk. This is commonly achieved by hedging against market risk. Hedging against market risk involves traders buying securities (meaning that they profit if the price of the securities increases), but hedging their position by simultaneously making investments that will generate a profit if the entire market drops (which would decrease the value of the stock initially purchased). For instance, investors may purchase shares in Company A, whilst simultaneously making an investment that will give rise to profits if the overall market in which Company A operates falls.

📖 **Principal Trading:** involves traders trading directly with clients, either selling securities that they already own to clients, or purchasing securities that are owned by clients.

📖 **Agency Trading:** involves clients transferring capital to a bank, which is then traded by the bank on the client's behalf.

📖 **Market-making:** traders quote the prices at which clients can buy or sell, based upon general trends in the market and their own opinion as to how the market is likely to change. The price at which trades are executed sets a general trend in the market for the prices of particular assets. Prices then fluctuate depending on the number of people buying or selling the assets. The role of traders in helping to determine these prices accordingly gave rise to their description as 'market-makers'.

📖 **Profit and Loss Account:** displays the net amount of money a trader has made or lost whilst trading.

📖 **Shorting:** Securities Lending (or Loan) desks will pay investors (typically large institutional investors) to borrow securities owned by the investors. These investors require collateral as protection in case the desk fails to return the securities on time when they are recalled (by the institutional investors). Traders can then access the borrowed securities and sell them either on their own accord (to generate profit) or on behalf of clients (and receive a commission) in the belief that they will be able to repurchase the securities at a later stage, at a cheaper price, in order to then return the securities to the investors from which they were borrowed. Investors may choose to lend stock to Securities Lending desks in such a manner if they wish to generate additional cash without having to actually sell their stock.

📖 **Going Long:** buying a security in the hope that the value will increase.

📖 **Bid – Offer Spread:** traders will quote a price at which a security can be bought and a price at which a security can be sold. The difference between these two prices is known as the bid-offer spread and this can determine a trader's profit margin. The liquidity of securities can affect their bid-offer spread.

Research

The Research department is almost always grouped together under the Markets division umbrella (Sales, Trading & Research), as Research analysts produce much of the information that the Sales and Trading teams use to inform their trade strategies and recommendations (to clients). Research teams are usually split up into two areas: (1) Fixed Income, Currencies & Commodities (FICC) and (2) Equities.

Research could involve conducting a detailed analysis of a particular asset class, company (or group of companies), market (including competitors and the level of market saturation) or industry (for instance providing an insight into industry trends or events that could or already have affected the performance of firms in that industry).

Research teams may produce projections of the future financial performance of companies (which could for instance help the Investment Banking Division to value a company for the purposes of an IPO); or estimations of future growth in particular asset classes, markets or regions (perhaps informing the investment decisions of traders or the advice offered by Sales people to their clients). This research is usually published in reports, either for internal teams and divisions, or clients.

📖 **Chinese Wall:** some of the information to which IBD bankers become privy must be kept private from the Sales and Trading teams. This is because these teams could otherwise potentially exploit the information to generate profits, which in turn could artificially manipulate the price of shares in the market. The barrier which is designed to stop the unethical free flow of information between different divisions within a bank is called the 'Chinese Wall' and its main objective is to prevent private information from being leaked, especially to the Markets division.

📖 **Insider Trading:** the buying or selling of a security based upon information procured that is not publicly available. This is a criminal offence as such action can give banks an unfair advantage and manipulate market prices. As such, banks must ensure sufficient controls are in place to enforce the 'Chinese Wall'.

Different Product Areas / Asset Classes

As mentioned, the Markets division is split into different departments. However, these departments are typically further split to cover particular products, sectors or regions (as is the case with the Investment Banking Division). This guide will cover the most commonly found sub-divisions, although you should be aware that some banks may split their divisions in different ways or may have additional arms such as Treasury or Prime Brokerage departments. Ensure that you research specifically into the banks to which you are applying so that you do not mistakenly reference a department using an incorrect name.

Fixed Income (Bonds)

The Fixed Income team deals with bonds issued by governments or corporations. This department is usually split into two teams: the Credit team, which focuses on corporations' bonds; and the Rates team, which focuses on government bonds. Bonds are generally traded over the counter (OTC).

📖 **Over The Counter (OTC):** the trading of securities through private dealer networks rather than on a public central exchange (such as the London Stock Exchange).

As mentioned in the *General Commercial Knowledge: Methods Of Financing* section, bonds are issued with a defined coupon rate (the interest that the bond issuer will pay to the purchasers of the bonds), which is often paid either annually, semi-annually or quarterly. The amount repaid once a bond matures is known as the principal amount (the stated price of the bond at the outset, though it is worthy to note bonds may be purchased at a discount or premium to the stated principle amount).

📖 **Maturity:** the time at which an issuer will pay the principal amount to bondholders. After this date, bondholders are no longer entitled to coupon payments from the issuer.

The price of a bond is calculated by summing the present value of all the future cash flows (coupon payments and the principal amount). Firstly, the estimated present value of each yearly coupon payment must be calculated:

$$\text{Present Value Of Cash Flow} = \frac{\text{Coupon Payment}}{(1 + \text{Interest Rate})^X}$$

X = the year for which the cash flow is being calculated. X = 1 when calculating the present value of the current year's cash flow. X = 2 for the estimated calculation of the 2nd year's cash flow and so on, right up until the year in which the final coupon payment is received.

As X increases, so does the number by which the coupon payment is divided, which in turn reduces the present value. As such, the further into the future that each cash flow is due to be received, the lower its calculated present value. This continuous reduction in value serves to represent the fact that the set coupon payment may be worth less in the future, partially due to the predicted effect of inflation and the fact that the money paid for the bond could potentially have been invested elsewhere had the bond not been purchased.

To calculate the price of a bond, the present values of each separate cash flow must be calculated then added together. The principal amount (due to be repaid when the bond matures) must then be similarly discounted and added to the calculation. The below example illustrates the price calculation for a bond that matures after 10 years (the '...' signifies that the present values for years 3-9 would also have to be calculated and added together). It is worthy to note that when you calculate the price of a bond, you are calculating the maximum price you would want to pay for the bond.

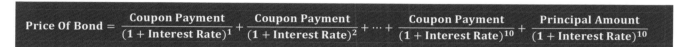

$$\textbf{Price Of Bond} = \frac{\textbf{Coupon Payment}}{(1 + \textbf{Interest Rate})^1} + \frac{\textbf{Coupon Payment}}{(1 + \textbf{Interest Rate})^2} + \cdots + \frac{\textbf{Coupon Payment}}{(1 + \textbf{Interest Rate})^{10}} + \frac{\textbf{Principal Amount}}{(1 + \textbf{Interest Rate})^{10}}$$

📖 **Yield:** in relation to bonds, this refers to the coupon (interest) payments bondholders receive (typically annually) expressed as a percentage of the price at which the bond is currently trading. Therefore, whilst the coupon rate is generally fixed, the yield % will change in line with fluctuations in the price at which the bond is trading. If the bond price increases, the fixed coupon rate will form a lower percentage of the (newly increased) price at which the bond is trading. As such, it can be stated that the yield of a bond moves inversely with price.

📖 **Yield To Maturity:** the anticipated return that the bondholder will receive by the time the bond matures (if they do not sell it before it reaches maturity). It is calculated based on its current price, coupon payments, face value and maturity date.

All bonds have credit ratings. The highest ratings denote the lowest perceived risk and are usually awarded to sovereign debt, whilst lower ratings are usually given to more speculative investments. All else being equal, usually the lower the rating, the higher the yield (interest payments), as this compensates investors for the higher risk of issuers defaulting (in which case, investors will not recoup their initial investment).

📖 **Yield Curve:** shows the relationship between interest rates and maturities by mapping out the interest rates bonds are paying across different maturities. The curve typically shows that the longer the time period before which the principal amount must be repaid (i.e. the further into the future the date of maturity is set), the higher the yield demanded by investors. This is because investors will likely require additional financial returns to compensate for the fact that they must wait a longer period before receiving the principal amount.

📖 **Callable Bonds:** this is a type of bond that has been issued on terms that entitle the issuer, under certain circumstances, to recall the bonds early through paying off all the debt in one early instalment.

📖 **Puttable Bonds:** this is a type of bond that has been issued on terms that entitle the bondholder (purchaser of the bond) to force the issuer to buy back the bond at the bondholder's discretion.

📖 **Perpetual Bond:** these pay interest indefinitely, but never mature. Issuers will not have to pay the principal amount to investors after a set time period. Instead, the bondholders expect to make a profit over time as the capital received through interest payments accumulates.

Currencies

The Foreign Exchange (FX) business involves banks and investors trading different currencies. Investors in the FX market include hedge funds, which are focused on profiting from volatility in the FX markets; large asset managers, which generally trade in large volumes and take more of a long-term view to profitability; and investors that require specific currencies to make particular investments. The rise of technology means that FX is often traded through the use of algorithms and electronic platforms. The FX business involves trading currencies over the counter (OTC), which means currencies are not traded on a central exchange.

The FX business plays a fundamental role in facilitating investment in different jurisdictions and the following scenarios provide examples of the circumstances under which the FX market may come into play. Investors may need to exchange their domestic currency for the foreign currency required to make a purchase in a different jurisdiction. A parent company may need to convert revenue generated by a subsidiary operating in a different region (assuming goods or services have been purchased using a different currency) into the currency used in the parent company's primary jurisdiction. Accordingly, the FX desk in a bank is likely to service a multitude of clients, rather than only clients from particular sectors.

Foreign exchange (FX) is the largest and most liquid market in the world. The liquidity of the market is advantageous for investors, as liquidity indicates there is ample opportunity to purchase or sell currencies (and thus investors will not end up stuck with an investment, unable to trade out of their position). Unlike the equities markets (which have set daily opening hours), the FX market is open 24 hours a day, 5 days a week. London is the main global hub for FX trading, although other major hubs include New York, Zurich, Tokyo, Frankfurt and Sydney. Some of the most traded currencies are the USD (United States Dollar), EUR (Euro), JPY (Japanese Yen), GBP (Pound Sterling), AUD (Australian Dollar) and the CHF (Swiss Franc).

Currencies are always quoted in pairs, as the price of any currency must be given relative to another currency. If you see GBP/USD = 1.70, this means the GBP is being used as the base currency and 1 GBP is currently worth 1.70 USD in the market.

📖 **Cable:** this is the term used traditionally to describe the GBP/USD pair on the trading floor. If a trader says: "I am long cable", this means that they believe the USD will depreciate in value relative to the GBP (meaning 1 GBP will in the future be worth more than 1.70 USD).

The FX market is driven by macroeconomic events. FX teams will generally focus on economic data such as the statistics discussed in the *Introduction To Economics: Macroeconomics* section when making trading decisions, in addition to other factors such as political events. However, there are often situations in which the FX market does not react as predicted and thus there is still an element of risk underpinning the decisions of FX teams.

Commodities

The commodities business involves the trading of physical assets. Examples include precious metals (such as gold and silver), energy (oil, gas and power) and agricultural produce (such as wheat or fruit). Many commodities are traded on a futures market, which simply means they are traded with the view that delivery will take place on a future date. However it is worth noting that the volume of commodities trading taking place in banks has started to diminish in light of regulations that have increased the costs of engaging in this form of trading. This is partly in recognition of the fact that the influence and input of banks in the commodities trading business has steadily increased the price of assets in general since 1990, creating artificially high prices that have consequently affected the profit margins of many other actors along the distribution chain.

Cash Equities

As mentioned, equities (also known as stocks or shares) are securities that afford the holders an ownership stake in the business that issued the securities. The owners of equity (shareholders) are therefore collectively the owners of the company, although they will not necessarily contribute to the day-to-day running of the company. The cash equities business essentially involves the issue and trading of shares.

Unlike fixed income securities, equities do not pay out a defined rate of interest to investors. Investors invest in equities because they believe that the business will flourish and as a result, the value of the shares will increase (as overall demand will rise for the shares), thus generating a profit for investors if and when they decide to sell their shares. They may also hope to receive healthy dividends whilst in possession of the shares, although dividends are generally distributed at businesses' discretion.

Pitching A Stock

Stocks can be pitched to clients in numerous ways and it is the job of Sales people to help determine the most effective method of pitching depending on the particular client and their specific objectives. Candidates may be asked to pitch a company's stock in an interview. This requires candidates to provide a recommendation as to whether a particular company's stock should be bought or sold. When doing so, candidates should ensure that they have researched into the company beforehand and have built a good understanding of the business. This could include for instance knowledge of where the company operates; who the CEO is (and their track record); the realistic price at which stocks could be purchased (this presumably will be the current spot (market) price, which should be checked on the day of the interview); and an estimation of the price at which the stock could subsequently be sold on (based on research and assumptions). Here are some of the considerations that could be taken into account for a stock pitch:

- **Macroeconomic Data:** general macroeconomic data could be used to support recommendations to buy or sell. Consider for instance whether governments have decided to offer subsidies to or regulate a certain industry in a manner that could affect the revenue of market participants. However, this would not necessarily differentiate a company from competitors and could instead only indicate that the industry as a whole may provide a good (or bad) investment option. Accordingly, any macroeconomic analysis should be supplemented with more specific (micro) analysis of a particular company.

- **Commercial News & Reports:** understanding and keeping up to date with news and developments relating to specific companies could indicate that companies' stock prices will move in a particular direction. Consider for instance whether any M&A activity or changes in management has taken place that is likely to increase the efficiency, scope or size (and thus value) of the company; consider whether sales figures (either for that specific company or for the industry in which the company operates) give rise to any patterns, such as a steady increase in demand; consider whether any negative press, such as reports of fraud, litigation or regulatory investigation, is likely to diminish the company's share price; consider whether the company has made any new investments which are likely to affect its future profitability (for instance investment into a new country or the development of a new product yet to be commercialised); and consider whether the company has announced plans to make any strategic changes, for instance closing down less profitable areas or improving their marketing and branding.

- **Metrics:** it may also be a good idea to assess metrics relating to financial performance, such as those included in the *General Financial Knowledge: Valuing A Business* section.

Derivatives

Financial assets can be traded in a multitude of ways. Investors can invest directly in shares or in exchange-traded funds (ETF), which track a number of stocks. With ETFs, investor returns depend on the performance of the group of stocks as a whole. Investors can purchase bonds directly or invest in an index (such as the FTSE 100 Index). One of the most common forms of trading different assets is via the use of derivatives. A derivative (also defined in the *General Commercial Knowledge: Strategic Challenges* section), as the name suggests, is a type of instrument that derives its value from the value of other assets (called underlying assets). Commonly used derivative contracts include forwards, futures and options.

Forwards & Futures

Forwards and futures are both contracts in which the seller of the derivative promises to sell an asset at a specific point in the future for a predetermined price (the 'strike price'). Forwards and futures are however traded in different ways.

📖 **Forwards:** contracts in which the parties involved agree to buy or sell assets at a specific point in the future for a predetermined price. Forwards are instruments that can be privately traded between two different parties over the counter (OTC), meaning that there is no need for a listing on a public exchange. The parties can personally negotiate terms that are tailored to suit their specific requirements and help fulfil their particular objectives, such as the date of delivery and the price to be paid in the future. Forwards give rise to some degree of counterparty risk, as if one party defaults (either on the promise to pay, or the promise to supply goods in the future) and becomes insolvent, the other party may lose out, subject to any remedy to which they may be entitled under insolvency law.

> **Futures:** contracts in which the parties involved agree to buy or sell assets at a specific point in the future for a predetermined price. In contrast to forwards however, futures are instruments traded on public exchanges. Futures contracts usually incorporate predetermined terms and conditions and thus, unlike forwards, are not individually negotiated and tailored to suit the specific needs of the parties involved. It is worthy to note that trading futures can involve lower counterparty risk than trading forwards, as futures are traded through a centralised clearing house that requires members to maintain sufficient funds to (at least partially) cover their debts.

It is important to note that anyone entering a forwards or futures agreement has a legal obligation to deliver whatever is promised by the predetermined date. For example, if the contract states that 100 barrels of oil must be delivered on the 20th September for $100 per barrel and on the 20th September the price is $90, the owner of the forward or future cannot renege on their agreement to buy purely because the price fluctuations in the market have resulted in the deal becoming less beneficial. In this sense, they are taking the risk when entering into the derivative contract that they will not end up worse off financially.

The use of forwards and futures is widespread. Organisations primarily utilise forwards and futures in order to ensure that they will receive sufficient quantities of required assets in the future and to lock in future prices in order to help manage and stabilise cash flows (through enabling more accurate future cost-predictions). For instance, airlines may purchase forwards to lock in the price of oil, thus enabling them to set future prices safe in the knowledge that their projected profit margins will be protected. Failure to utilise derivative contracts could ultimately expose them to significant cost increases (which may end up destroying profit margins) if, for instance, an unforeseen macroeconomic shock occurs (such as a crisis that affects the supply, and thus the price of oil).

Options

Options serve a similar purpose to forwards and futures, in the sense that they could also, for instance, entitle the purchaser to purchase an asset at a specified price (the 'strike price') on a predetermined future date. However, options can be more beneficial to the holder in the sense that, unlike futures or forwards, the contract for an option does not obligate the holder of the option to actually take up the option when the relevant date arrives. Instead, the contract gives them the option, at their own discretion, to go ahead with the transaction. As such, options are typically more expensive than futures or forwards. There are two main types of options: call options and put options.

> **Call Options:** these give the purchaser the option (but confer no obligation upon them) to buy an underlying asset in the future at a predetermined price.

> **Put Options:** these give the purchaser the option (but confer no obligation upon them) to sell an underlying asset in the future at a predetermined price.

If the market price happens to decrease by the time the predetermined date at which the option may be taken up arrives, the holder of the option can simply refrain from exercising their option and instead purchase the desired asset directly from the market at its current (potentially cheaper) price. This additional benefit favours the purchaser of the option and as such, the seller of the option under such circumstances would usually require the purchaser to pay a premium.

For example, if you purchase a call option that entitles you to buy 1000 of Company A's shares for £10 each in 1 month's time, but in a month, the market price is actually £8 per share, you can choose not to exercise (take up) the option and instead purchase the shares at the cheaper price. However, if Company A's shares happen to be trading for £12 each in a month's time, you can exercise the option and take advantage of the £2 saving per share. In this example, if the market price of the shares is above £10 while the option is still active, then the option is described as being 'in the money' as it entitles the (call) option holder to purchase the shares at a price that is lower than the market price. Conversely, if the option was a put option, it would be described as 'in the money' if it entitled the seller to sell at a price that is higher than the market price.

It can be important to know some of the key factors that may influence the price of an option, however a full understanding of the factors is not typically expected of you at the interview stage. Some of these factors are included in the below table.

Key Factors	Price of Call Option	Price of Put Option
Current price of underlying asset increases	Increases	Decreases
The price at which the option entitles the purchaser to purchase the underlying asset in the future (if so they wish) increases	Deceases	Increases
Market volatility increases	Increases	Increases
The length of time for which the option remains active increases	Increases	Increases

Swaps

A swap is a derivative that involves two counterparties agreeing to exchange (swap) a series of future cash flow streams to which they are entitled by virtue of their ownership of particular securities (for example, the interest payments to which they are entitled by virtue of their ownership of bonds).

Typically, the value of one series of cash flow streams involved in the swap is uncertain at the outset. Its value could for instance change in line with macroeconomic changes or developments in the market. For example, the value of one cash flow stream being swapped may be linked to: the change in price of shares or a change in the amount of the dividends paid to holders of the shares (an equity swap) or a floating interest rate (an interest rate swap).

Through enabling parties that are due to receive uncertain amounts of money to trade in the uncertainty for fixed payments, swaps facilitate more accurate budgeting through enabling parties to fix the value of future cash flows that they are due to receive. This can also help parties to mitigate (hedge against) the risk of receiving less money than expected if the market moves adversely. Conversely, parties entitled to a stream of cash flows with a fixed value may wish to speculate, trading in the right to receive payments of a predetermined value in the belief that the market may move in a manner that will result in them receiving cash flows that exceed the value of the fixed cash flows to which they would otherwise have been entitled.

Market Sizing & Brainteasers

Market sizing questions and brainteasers are designed to assess the thought process you follow and logic you apply in order to reach a final answer. When answering market sizing/brainteaser questions, you are not generally expected to reach a final numerical answer that is particularly close (or equal) to the true value (although you must make *reasonable/rational* numerical estimations along the way).

Examples of questions you may be asked

1. What is the size of the potential customer base of a dating website?

2. How many footballs could fill up Wembley Stadium?

3. How many leaves are there on a tree?

4. How heavy is the building we are sitting in?

5. How many shoes are sold in India every year?

6. How many cars are there on average at any one time in the UK every year?

7. How much is the Houses of Parliament worth?

Your Thought Process

Ensure that you think out loud. Make the interviewer aware of your thought process and carefully explain all your assumptions and calculations throughout. These types of questions are also typically designed to test how well you react to unexpected questions under pressure, as this is something that investment bankers may have to do regularly when working with clients.

Pragmatism vs. Accuracy

Strike a balance between pragmatism and accuracy. Round up numbers/work with averages when necessary to ensure you can make calculations mentally if required.

- Perhaps round some numbers up and some down in order to ensure you remain as accurate as possible.

- For instance, instead of including 19% in your calculations, round it up to 20% for the sake of simplifying the calculations, instead of taking 58 million as a size of the population, round it up to 60 million (again remember that it is not the final number that matters).

If the interviewer will let you, validate your proposed process of reaching a conclusion with the interviewer before plugging in your estimations. You could also see if the interviewer is willing to validate your estimations along the way, as if the interviewer feels your estimations are fair, at least you know you are along the right track.

Sanity Check

A majorly inaccurate estimation at the beginning of a set of calculations could completely diminish the accuracy of your final figure, even if a majority of the subsequent estimations are realistic. Consistently make sanity checks to ensure your estimations are leading you towards a conclusion that is not wholly illogical.

> 📖 **Sanity Check:** once you have made a few estimations and started to make calculations, performing a 'sanity check' means assessing whether the results of those calculations vaguely relate to the figure that common sense would dictate could be correct. A sanity check could for instance indicate you have missed 0's along the way, or massively over or underestimated the size of the market or its specific segment.

When you first arrive at a final number, you should use your business judgement to determine whether that number is realistic. Your intuition should tell you whether the number seems either too big or too small. You should then be able to verify your assumptions, indicate those that may have led to the final under/over-estimation and carefully consider whether more appropriate estimations can replace any of your existing estimations in order to give you a more realistic and logical final number. Once you have corrected and restated your assumptions to the interviewer, you may then be asked to perform the calculations again.

Break The Question Down

One way to approach market sizing questions is to break the question down into little problems and then input your estimations into a tree to structure your problem. If you have 20 minutes to solve a problem, do not make a couple of rushed calculations and give your estimation within the first 2 minutes. The more time you have, the more you should try to break down the problem and demonstrate to the interviewer that you are able to think flexibly, make informed assumptions and recognise and consider a wide range of variables.

Variables

Note that the nature of market sizing/brainteaser questions can vary enormously. There is no way that you can possibly prepare for every type of question in advance. However, getting to grips with the different variables that exist in a variety of contacts can help you to develop your ability to think flexibly.

- If you are asked how many chocolate bars are purchased in England annually, remember to take into account chocolate bars purchased by *tourists* within the UK rather than simply estimating the proportion of the English population that purchases chocolate bars.

- If asked how many jackets Tesco sells annually, consider the proportion of Tesco stores that sell clothing. If asked how many cars are sold by BMW in the UK every year, does this mean only cars branded with the BMW logo, or cars produced by BMW (for instance, Minis)?

- If asked about a hypothetical market, you could start by considering which industries already provide for a similar end-goal. For instance, if asked what the potential market for teleportation would be, you could consider the current market for long-haul flights as your starting point (as both teleportation and long-haul flights relate to people wanting to travel). You could then base your estimates on the market for long-haul flights, whilst acknowledging that factors such as price, accessibility and safety would impact upon the estimations.

Example: Market Sizing

Interviewer: How much *milk* does Starbucks use on a typical *working* day in the UK?

You (interviewee): Ok, can I please have a minute to think about how best to break down this problem?

Interviewer: Yes, of course.

You (interviewee):

- For the sake of the analysis, I will assume that there are approximately 1000 Starbucks stores across the UK. I am aware that these stories vary in size, but I will perform calculations based on a sample average-sized store. I am assuming that this sample store opens at 7am and closes at 7pm on the average working day (12 hours of trading per working day).

- I will proceed on the basis that there are typically 2 cash registers operating at any one time and each serves, on average, one customer per minute. This average is based upon the assumption that more than 1 customer per minute is served during busy periods (for instance the mornings) and fewer at other times. We therefore have 2 customers per minute (remember, we have assumed there are 2 cash registers operating simultaneously) x 60 minutes x 12 hours, giving us 1440 customers per day.

- I am aware that not every customer will buy drinks that include milk (for instance soft drinks and black coffee). However, some customers will also make multiple purchases (for instance, if they are buying drinks for other people). I will therefore proceed under the assumption that 1440 drinks requiring milk are sold on average in each Starbucks store every day. I will also assume that the average sized drink is medium (and medium drinks are approximately 480 millilitres (ml) in size), and that milk accounts for 25% of the volume (i.e. 120ml per drink).

- Finally, we can multiply the number of drinks requiring milk that are sold on average per day (1440) by the average amount of milk contained within each of these drinks (120ml), then multiply this figure by the estimated number of Starbucks stores in the UK (1000). You could write down your calculations (see below).

Interviewer: Do you think 172,800 litres is a realistic estimate?

You (interviewee):

- As the analysis comprises of a wide range of assumptions, there is a realistic chance that the estimate may differ from the actual figure. The assumption that 1000 stores exist around the UK is based solely on intuition, as are the assumptions relating to the average number of drinks requiring milk that are sold and the average amount of milk that goes into each drink. Opening hours will vary, as will the number of cash registers. During peak times, the queues in stores may force staff to work faster and more efficiently (and there may be some staff that work particularly slowly, regardless of the setting). Furthermore, the average number of drinks sold may change in correlation with seasons (i.e. more hot, milky drinks may be sold in the winter) or with the release of new products/promotions (e.g. a new brand of espresso/the launch of the Starbucks loyalty card).

As part of your analysis, you could have further segmented Starbucks stores. For instance, you could have given estimates for small stores in big cities (for instance in train stations), large stores in big cities, small regional stores (e.g. in regional towns) and large regional stores (e.g. in motorway service stations).

You could then make estimations that are more tailored to the likely volume of relevant drink sales within those different segments. You could follow this by estimating the number of stores within each segment and then come up with a total figure. The decision to segment must be considered in light of the particular facts you are facing and the time limit you are given (if you are given a time limit).

Example: Brainteaser

Interviewer: How many footballs could you fit into Wembley Stadium?

You (interviewee): Ok, can I please have a minute to think about how best to break down this problem?

Interviewer: Yes, of course

You (interviewee):

To start off with, I will make the following assumptions about Wembley Stadium:

1. The stadium is set up for a football match (as opposed to a concert, in which case the stage and props might take up additional space, thus reducing the number of footballs that could fit into the stadium) and there are no people in the stadium;

2. The stadium is a cuboid-like structure (i.e. any rounded/sloping structural edges will be ignored). This assumption will make it easier to perform the necessary calculations to estimate its volume.

I will now make the following estimations in order to calculate the approximate volume of Wembley Stadium:

1. The football pitch is approximately 100 metres long and 70 meters wide and there is around 10 metres of space between the pitch and the seats;

2. There are approximately 80 rows of seats in each stand of the stadium. Each row is approximately 1 metre deep and adds approximately ½ metre of height. The top row of seats is 10 metres below the roof. This makes the height of the stadium approximately 50 metres;

3. The space between the pitch and the seats, the non-seating areas (e.g. gangways) and the perimeter of the stadium (e.g. the bars, restaurants and offices etc.) add approximately 20 metres of depth to each side.

This gives us the following estimated dimensions to work with:

1. **Stadium length of 300 metres**: 100m (pitch) + 160m (seats either side of the pitch) + 40m (extras either side of pitch) = 300m

2. **Stadium width of 270 metres:** 70m (pitch) + 160m (seats either side of the pitch) + 40m (extras either side of pitch) = 270 metres

3. **Stadium height of 50 metres:** 40m (seats) + 10m (space above seats) = 50 metres

4. **Stadium volume of 4,050,000 cubic metres:** 300m x 270m x 50m

I will initially treat footballs as if they are cubes with the same diameter as an average football. This will allow me to make a direct division of volumes to obtain the answer (the estimated volume of Wembley Stadium divided by the estimated volume of a football). Based on the assumption that the diameter of an average football is 0.2 metres, the volume of a single "football" would be 0.008 metres^3 (0.2 x 0.2 x 0.2).

This suggests that the number of footballs that could fit inside a completely empty Wembley Stadium is: 4,050,000/0.008 = **506,250,000** footballs.

However, this does not take into account the fact that there are numerous seats, internal walls and windows, restaurant/bar fixtures and fittings, ticket offices, windows, pillars etc. inside the stadium, which reduce the space available. In addition, more spherical balls could fit inside the stadium than solid cubes.

Accordingly, I will make the following estimations and adjustments:

1. The seats take up approximately 5% of the stadium;

2. If I were to estimate the amount of non-space in a much smaller structure with which I am more familiar with (for instance, a restaurant or a house) I would say that there is around 10% non-space. Applying this logic to a stadium, I will therefore estimate that the internal walls, pillars, windows, fixtures and fittings take up another 10% of the stadium; and

3. 5% more spherical balls than solid cubes (with identical diameters) could fit inside the stadium (as spherical balls have a smaller volume than cubes with identical diameters).

The figure should be reduced by 10% (5% uplift + 10% uplift - 5% reduction), giving us the estimated conclusion that approximately **455,625,000 footballs could fit inside Wembley Stadium.**

In an interview, you may be given a pen and paper to use. If this is the case, use it! If relevant, draw a picture of the object you are analysing (e.g. a stadium or office building) and/or map out your thought process as a diagram (see the framework below). This will not only help you to remember your estimations, but will also help the interviewer to follow your thought process.

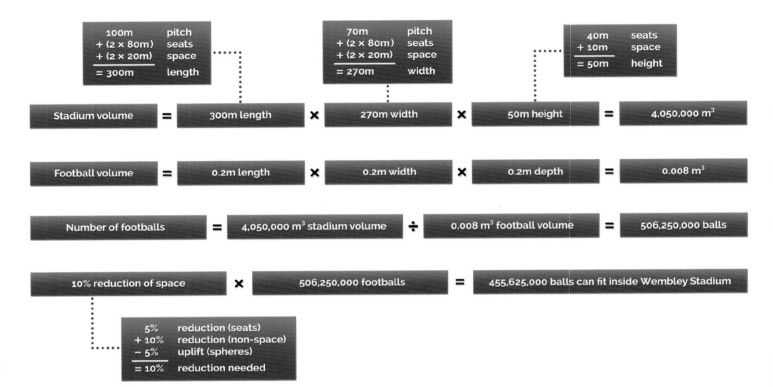

Assumptions

Only make assumptions for the following reasons: (1) to very briefly demonstrate that you are considering every detail; or (2) if they really do help answer the question. Interviewers are much more interested in the logic and reasoning that underpin your answers (including your thought process) than the specific conditions/assumptions you choose to adopt (e.g. whether the stadium is set up for a football match or concert, whether there are people in the stadium etc.). The best way to think of this is to imagine the interviewer asking "what is the relevance of this assumption and how does it influence your logic/thought process?" If you cannot give a *good* answer, then the assumption is probably not needed.

To place this advice in context, let's consider the assumptions made in relation to the Wembley Stadium example. The assumption that the stadium is set up for football match demonstrated that I am able to consider a variety of variables that could impact on the answer and make a reasonable judgment call. The decision to treat the stadium as if it were a cuboid and treating footballs as cubes enabled me to reach a final answer (based on the various estimations made) using fairly simple arithmetic.

Whilst assumptions relate more to the conditions you adopt and the logic you follow when considering a particular question, estimations are used to come up with values that you can then input into calculations. Try not to make blind (i.e. random/ill considered) estimations. Justify as many of the estimations/assumptions in your answer as possible. The only way you are likely to fall down when making estimations is if your estimations are clearly unfounded (e.g. estimating that a football pitch is 20 metres long).

Using a pen and paper can also help you when making more complicated calculations. You must try to find a balance between being detailed in your logic and estimations and using numbers that you will be able to deal with comfortably under pressure. You may have to do calculations without a calculator during an assessment day. Where this is the case, consider ensuring that the numbers you estimate are fairly easy to deal with and/or practice making complex calculations without a calculator beforehand. Consider these two examples:

- Instead of trying to divide the volume of the stadium by 0.008 metres^3 (the estimated volume of a football), you could round up the size of a football to 0.01 metres^3. This would make the division easier to calculate in your head under pressure.

- When trying to calculate the volume of the stadium based on the estimated dimensions (300m x 270m x 50m) you could break down the calculation into more digestible stages. Start by removing the four 0s, leaving you with 3 x 27 x 5. Next, (if needed) break this down further. 3 x 27 = 81, so we need to calculate 81 x 5. 81 x 5 can be broken down as follows: 8 x 5 = 40 → 80 x 5 = 400 → 81 x 5 = 405. Finally, you add back the four 0s (i.e. multiply by a factor of 10,000) that you originally removed, leaving you with **4,050,000**.

Microsoft Excel

You will most likely work frequently with Microsoft Excel if you are working in the financial services industry. It will be the key software you will use to build financial models, analyse cash flows (and projected cash flows) and carry out various types of analysis for clients/supervisors. You will likely receive some training at the start of an internship or career, but it is advisable to develop your Microsoft Excel skills in advance to ensure you can work efficiently and effectively from the outset.

This is only a basic guide to some of the most commonly used Microsoft Excel functions, formulas and shortcuts. To expand and deepen your understanding, you should undertake further study. Breaking Into Wall Street's 'Excellence With Excel' course is highly recommended. It is worth noting that slightly different commands and terminology may apply to different versions of Microsoft Excel (for instance, Microsoft Excel for Mac/PC, older versions and versions released in different countries). If this is the case, supplement the information contained in this section with additional research in order to ensure you are following the correct instructions and using the correct formulas. Note that a majority of financial services firms use PCs, so the information in this section relates primarily to PC keyboards and PC versions of Microsoft Excel. The screenshots in this section are used with permission from Microsoft.

Navigation & Editing

Many professionals barely use the mouse when working with Microsoft Excel. Pretty much anything you can do with a mouse click can be done using only the keyboard. With practice, the use of shortcuts will become more intuitive and using only the keyboard can become a more efficient way of working.

Navigating Around The Worksheet

`Ctrl + End`: move to the last used cell of the current worksheet (i.e. the lowest row of the rightmost column).

`Home`: return to the first cell of the current row in a worksheet.

`Ctrl + Tab`: switch to the next open workbook.

`Ctrl + PgDown` / `Ctrl + PgUp`: switch to the next / previous worksheet.

📖 **Microsoft Excel Worksheet:** a single spreadsheet comprised of rows and columns.

📖 **Microsoft Excel Workbook:** a collection of one or more worksheets within the same document.

Editing Cells, Rows & Columns

`Ctrl + Home` followed by `Ctrl+Shift+End`: select the entire range of cells in the worksheet that contain data.

`Ctrl + Space`: select the entire column that you are currently working in.

`Shift + Space`: select the entire row that you are currently working in.

`Ctrl + + (plus sign)`: insert new row / column (depending on whether you have selected an entire row or column before making the command). The new row (column) will appear above (to the left of) the one selected.

`Ctrl + - (minus sign)`: delete the row or column that you have selected.

`F2`: if you select a cell and press F2, all the cells in the Worksheet that are referenced within the formula inside the selected cell will be highlighted.

`Ctrl + T`: convert the selected cells into a table.

Copying & Pasting

`Ctrl + D`: copy the contents and format of the first cell in the selected range into the cells below. If more than one column is selected, the contents of the topmost cell in each column will be copied downwards. This would usually be used to copy a formula from one cell into other cells.

`Ctrl + Shift + V`: open the "Paste Special" option once information has been copied onto the clipboard. When you copy a cell that contains a formula, then select another cell and click Paste, the formula will be duplicated into the newly selected cell. Paste Special however gives you additional options, including the option to paste the actual number contained within the original cell (not the formula itself).

Formatting

Number Formatting

- Microsoft Excel may sometimes format cells in ways that you do not intend it to. For instance, when inserting a date into a cell, instead of displaying 07/09/2015, Microsoft Excel may instead display the numbers in a different format. The same goes for decimals and percentages (etc.). You can ensure that cells display values as you intend them to by right clicking the relevant cell(s), selecting the 'Format Cells' option, then selecting your desired format. Cells will then update accordingly.

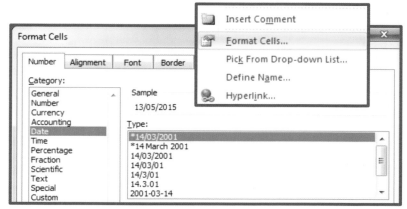

- Below are some useful keyboard shortcuts you can use when formatting cell values:

   Ctrl + Shift + 1 : if you have a value that is formatted in a particular way (e.g. currency, percentage etc.), this command will change that value to a simple number (e.g. £100.00 becomes 100.00, 100% becomes 1.00 etc.).

   Ctrl + Shift + 4 : adds a currency sign to the cell value (the currency will depend on the Microsoft Excel version).

   Ctrl + Shift + 5 : converts the value into its percentage equivalent (0.2 would be 20%, 1 would be 100% etc.).

Filtering Data

- You can use Microsoft Excel to filter data so that only the values you are interested in are displayed. To filter your data, select the top cell of a chosen column and then click 'Filter' on the Data tab. A small arrow will appear on the bottom right corner of the selected cell.

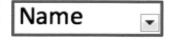

- Clicking on the arrow will give you the option to choose which data in the relevant column you would like to filter out. For example, if you have a column containing the names of various employees, you could apply the filtering function to the column in order to exclude from your data the rows corresponding to the names of some of the employees (you do this by clicking the small arrow then deselecting the relevant employee names).

Sorting Data

- Microsoft Excel can make it easier for you to sort data (for instance, from smallest to largest if cells contain numbers, or in alphabetical order if cells contain letters).

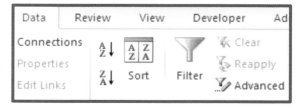

- To sort your data, select the top cell of a chosen column and then click 'Sort' on the Data tab. This will give you different options for sorting your data.

Grouping & Hiding Columns / Rows

- The Hide function is useful if you want to display only the columns/rows in your worksheet that are relevant to your analysis. To hide data, select the column(s)/row(s) you want to hide, then right click and select Hide. To unhide those column(s)/row(s), select the columns/rows that are on either side of the hidden column(s)/row(s), then right click and select Unhide.

- The Group function can also be a useful tool to help you organise and work more efficiently with your spreadsheet. To group cells, first select the columns/rows you wish to group, then select the 'Group' option from the Data tab. Once you have grouped columns/rows, the numbers 1 and 2 will appear on the top left corner of the worksheet (see below). Click option 1 to hide the grouped columns/rows and option 2 to expand them.

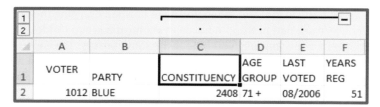
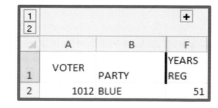

Freezing Panes

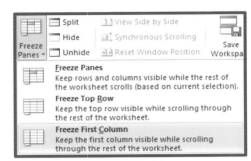

- Freezing panes can come in useful when your dataset contains hundreds of rows and/or columns and you need to reference a particular row or column regardless of where within the worksheet you are working. For instance, let us assume that the first row contains headings that specify which type of data should appear in each corresponding column. If you freeze the first row, no matter how far you subsequently scroll down, the entries in that first row will be displayed at the top of the area of the spreadsheet visible on your screen.

- To freeze a column or row, select the relevant column/row and then click Freeze Panes on the View tab. If you select an entire row, all the rows above it (not including the selected row) will freeze. If you select an entire column, all the columns to the left of it (not including the selected column) will freeze. If you select a particular cell, all the rows above it and the columns to the left of it will freeze.

Leaving Comments

- It may be useful to leave comments in spreadsheets to ensure that other users can understand the contents.

- To do this, first select the cell to which you would like to attach a comment, then click New under the Review tab. A yellow box will open, giving you space to leave a comment. Once you have left a comment, a red arrow will appear in the top right corner of the cell to indicate to other users that upon clicking that cell, a comment will appear.

Graphs & Charts

- Microsoft Excel provides a wide range of options for visualising data. To create a graph/chart, select the relevant data, then click the Inset tab and select the type of graph/ chart you would like to use (Column, Line, Pie, Bar etc.).

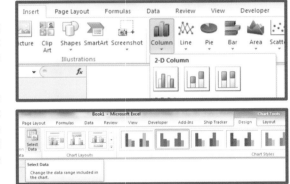

- Microsoft Excel tries to automatically determine which data should be displayed on the X-axis and Y-axis. If the data does not display in the way you intend it to once the graph/chart has been created, go to the Design tab under the Chart Tools ribbon and click Select Data. From here you can modify the way in which the graph/chart plots your data.

Using Microsoft Excel Without A Mouse

Almost every Microsoft Excel function/formula can be accessed through 'alt' shortcuts. Once you press alt, you can then press combinations of letters and numbers (depending on what you want to achieve) that enable you to access the functions contained within the ribbon menus. For example, if you select two cells next to each other and then click alt followed by H, M and C (the shortcuts for Home → Merge → Merge and Centre), the two cells will merge. Developing your ability to use Microsoft Excel without a mouse can (in time) greatly improve your efficiency. Why not practise by unplugging your mouse so that you *have* to use alt shortcuts.

Formulas

Inserting, Pasting & Moving Formulas

Selecting Cells

- If you want to refer to particular cells in a formula/calculation, you can either type out the specific cell references that you want to include (e.g. 'A1') or click the relevant cells.

- You can also select *arrays* (groups) of cells that you wish to include in a particular formula/calculation. You can do this by, for instance, typing in the start of the formula (e.g. '=SUM(') then clicking one cell and dragging the cursor across the other cells that you wish to include in the particular array. When you have finished dragging the cursor over the relevant cells and have let go of the mouse/track pad button, those cells will form a group ('ARRAY1'). If you then want to insert an additional group of cells into the formula, you repeat the same process (i.e. select the additional range of cells). The additional range of cells will form a second group ('ARRAY2') and so on. One array of cells will display in a formula as two cell references separated by a colon, e.g. 'A1:10'. =SUM(A1:A10) would sum A1, A2, A3…A10, whilst =SUM(A1:B10) would calculate *all* of the values in cells A1-A10 *and* B1-B10.

Autocomplete Formula/Function Name

- If you type the start of a formula into a cell (for example =HL) and then press Tab, the formula (e.g. **=HLOOKUP**) will automatically enter into the cell, saving you from having to enter in the entire formula manually. If more than one formula begins with the characters that you enter into the cell, then pressing Tab will insert into the cell whichever relevant formula comes first alphabetically.

Pasting Formulas Into Different Cells

- If you click and hold the bottom right corner of a cell that contains a formula, then drag the cursor down/across cells in the same column/row, the formula in the first cell will appear in each of the newly selected cells (relative to its new position). This function is applicable not only to formulas, but also to days of the week, months, numerical patterns etc. For instance, if you type 'Monday' into a cell and then drag the corner of the cell down, each subsequent cell will display the day of the week that follows the day displayed in the cell above. If you type '1' into a cell, '3' into the cell below, then highlight both cells and drag the corner of the bottom cell down, Excel will maintain the pattern of displaying only odd numbers in subsequent cells.

Relative/Absolute Reference Types

- The default position in Microsoft Excel is that the 'relative reference type' applies when pasting formulas into different cells. This means that a formula will change when pasted into new cells, relative to its new location. For instance, if the formula in cell C1 is **=A1*B1** and you copy this formula into cell C2, the pasted formula will change to **=A2*B2**. You can instead opt to use the 'absolute reference type' when copying a formula into a different cell. This will mean that the formula copied into a different cell will appear in exactly the same form regardless of which cell you paste it into. To change the reference type for a formula contained within a cell, firstly double click the cell containing the relevant formula so that the formula pops up (or click the cell so that the formula appears in the formula bar under the Ribbon). Next, click the part of the formula that you would like to change. Pressing F4 (cmd+T for Mac) then lets you cycle through the different reference types.

- You may also want to use a formula that uses a combination of absolute and relative reference types. For instance, in the example to the right, column B displays the net prices of products and cell D1 displays the fixed VAT rate applicable to all sales. To calculate the specific amount of VAT chargeable on each price, you would require one part of the formula to remain the same, regardless of the position of the formula (i.e. you would always want it to reference cell D1). You would however want the other part of the formula to change relative to its position (i.e. relative to the product price that the formula is next to).

VLOOKUP		fx	=$D$1*B2	
	A	B	C	D
1	Product	Price	VAT	0.22
2	Pen	£2.50	=$D$1*B2	
3	Pencil	£1.50		
4	Table	£25.60		
5	Chair	£12.30		
6	Notebook	£0.90		

- You can achieve this by placing the $ sign in front of both the letter and the number of the cell you wish to remain fixed in the formula. In this example, $D$1 is used as we want to include the value in cell D1 in the formula regardless of the formula's position. In contrast, the cell multiplied by D1 will continue to change relative to the position of the formula, ensuring that each different price is multiplied by the fixed VAT rate.

VLOOKUP		fx	=$D$1*B5	
	A	B	C	D
1	Product	Price	VAT	0.22
2	Pen	£2.50	£0.55	
3	Pencil	£1.50	£0.33	
4	Table	£25.60	£5.63	
5	Chair	£12.30	=$D$1*B5	
6	Notebook	£0.90	£0.20	

Calculations

=SUM(A1,B1,C1...) / **=A1-B1-C1...** sum / subtract cell values

=PRODUCT(A1,A2) / **=A1/A2** multiply / divide cell values

=AVERAGE(A1:A10) / **=MEDIAN(A1:A10)** calculate the average / median of the specified values

=MIN(A1:A10) / **=MAX(A1:A10)** calculate the minimum / maximum value contained within selected cells

=COUNT(A1:A100) / **=COUNTA(A1:A100)** counting the number of cells containing numbers / data

- **=COUNT** enables you to calculate the number of cells in a specified range that contain any numbers. You can select the cells (including entire rows and/or columns) that you would like the formula to consider. In the above example, the formula would count the number of cells between (and including) A1 and A100 that contain numbers. Note that if you want to find the number of cells containing letters and/or symbols (or a combination of letters, symbols and numbers), replace **COUNT** with **COUNTA**.

=SUMPRODUCT(array1,array2...) summing the products of corresponding cells

- You can combine 'SUM' and 'PRODUCT' into the same formula in order to multiply together corresponding cells and calculate the sum of the products. For instance, the above formula will calculate the product of the 1st value in array 1 (column D) with the 1st value in array 2 (column E), then the 2nd value in array 1 with the second value in array 2 (and so on). It then calculates the sum of the totals of these calculations.

- Let us take the formula =SUMPRODUCT(ARRAY1,ARRAY2). If you select cells D2, D3, D4 and D5 to form ARRAY1, then cells E2, E3, E4 and E5 to form ARRAY2, the formula will become =SUMPRODUCT(D2:D5,E2:E5).

- This formula will then calculate (D2 x E2) + (D3 x E3) + (D4 x E4) + (D5 x E5), as illustrated in the print screen on the right. Note that each array must contain the same number of cells, as the formula is dependent on each cell value having a corresponding cell value.

f_x	=SUMPRODUCT(D2:D5,E2:E5)
D	**E**
Price	**Quantity Sold**
£10.00	1
£5.00	5
£20.00	2
£2.00	10
Total Revenue	£95.00

Logical Operators

=IF(logical_test, [value_if_true], [value_if_false]) obtaining results that are dependent on test criteria

- This function gives you a result that is dependent upon the criteria set by you in the **'logical_test'** field and the data you enter into the **'[value_if_true]'** and **'[value_if_false]'** boxes.

- To illustrate this formula, we have chosen the following example. If you have a set of exam results and the pass mark is 40%, you could use this formula to provide you with a list of the students that passed and failed. Using the formula =IF(D2>39,"Pass","Fail") would mean that the word "Pass" will display in the selected cell if the grade listed in D2 is greater than 39 and "Fail" will display if the grade listed is 39 or below.

f_x	=IF(D2>39,"Pass","Fail")
D	**E**
Grade	**Result**
65	Pass
34	Fail
44	Pass
28	Fail

- Here are some useful commands that you may wish to include as part of your **'logical_test'**: = (equal to), > (greater than), < (less than), >= (greater than or equal to), <= (less than or equal to), <> (not equal to).

=COUNTIF(range, criteria) counting the number of cells that contain a specified piece of data

- This function will search through the cells that you have selected/specified and tell you how many of these cells contain the data that you have asked it to focus upon. Whilst **=COUNT/=COUNTA** simply tell you the number of cells containing (any) data, **=COUNTIF** allows you to be more specific about what you are looking for (i.e. a specific number or word).

- In the formula in the example to the right, D2:D6 shows that cells D2 through to D6 have been selected. This is then followed by a comma and "Pass", which tells the formula to calculate the number of cells in that selected area that contain the word "Pass" (the answer being 3). To calculate the total number of fails, the same formula will be used, but with the word "Fail" in place of "Pass".

f_x	=COUNTIF(D2:D6, "Pass")
C	**D**
Grade	**Result**
Wojciech	Pass
Jake	Fail
Sean	Pass
Frida	Fail
Tomisin	Pass
Total Pass	3
Total Fail	2

=SUMIF(range, criteria, [sum_range]) summing the values within cells that meet your specified criteria

- We could use this formula to find the total revenue generated by a specific product (in this example, sandwiches). In the formula, cells C2 to C8 have first been selected, then the word "Sandwich" has been entered (after a comma) to denote that only rows containing the word 'Sandwich' are relevant to the search. Finally, the cells containing the corresponding numbers that you wish to sum are highlighted (the prices are contained in cells D2 to D8).

- To clarify, whilst **COUNTIF** could be used to calculate the *number* of sandwiches sold, **SUMIF** can be used to calculate the sum of the revenue generated from all the sandwiches sold.

f_x	=SUMIF(C2:C8,"Sandwich",D2:D8)
C	**D**
Product	**Revenue**
Sandwich	£2.00
Drink	£1.00
Chocolate	£1.00
Drink	£3.00
Chocolate	£1.00
Sandwich	£3.50
Drink	£2.00
Revenue from sandwiches	£5.50

Lookup Functions

=VLOOKUP(lookup_value, table_array, col_index_number, [range_lookup])

Search for a specified value in the leftmost column of a selected group of cells, then find a corresponding value on the same row as the cell containing that specified value

- 'V' stands for vertical, as this formula is used to search out data contained vertically down a column. To illustrate the usefulness of the formula, a fictitious shop record of customer purchases has been created (see the below print screen). Rather than the 5 orders presented below, pretend that thousands of orders have been received. If a customer enters the shop wanting a refund, but only has their order number with them, this formula could enable the shop assistant to search out particular details about that customer and what they purchased without having to scroll through thousands of entries. In this example, we want to find the price paid.

- In the '**lookup_value**' section of the formula, you must type in the value that you would like to base your search upon. In this example, the customer's ID (under the Order ID Search heading) has been entered into the cell. The nature of this formula means that your initial search must involve data that is contained within the leftmost column of the relevant group of cells (i.e. the Order ID column).

fx	=VLOOKUP(D9,D2:G6,4,FALSE)		
D	**E**	**F**	**G**
Order ID	**Customer name**	**Product**	**Price Paid**
101011	Jake	Notepad	£5.00
101012	Wojciech	Pencils	£3.00
101013	Frida	Pens	£6.00
101014	Sean	Calculator	£20.00
101015	Tomisin	Highlighters	£8.00
Order ID Search	**Price Paid**		
101013	£6.00		

- Next, in the '**table_array**' section of the formula, you select the group of cells within which you would like the formula to search. In this example, cells D2 to G6 have been selected as these contain all the information about customer orders.

- In the '**col_index_number**' section of the formula, you must detail the specific column from which you would like to extract particular data. In the above example, '4' has been inputted, as the price paid is in column 4 and this is the information we would like to find.

- The final element of the formula, '**range_lookup**', is an optional criterion. If you input the word 'FALSE' into the formula, then it will only return a value (i.e. the price paid) if your search returns an exact match (i.e. the customer order number that you enter exists somewhere down the Order ID column). If instead of 'FALSE" you input 'TRUE', then if your search does not find an exact match (i.e. the order number does not exist), the formula will instead use the next lowest value in the column (i.e. Order ID 101012 instead of 101013).

=HLOOKUP(lookup_value, table_array, row_index_number, [range_lookup])

Search for a specified value in the top row of a selected group of cells, then find a corresponding value in the same column as the cell containing that specified value

- This function is similar in nature to VLOOKUP. 'H' stands for horizontal, as this formula is used to search out data horizontally along a row. To illustrate this function, the same data will be used, but in a different format.

fx	=HLOOKUP(C7,D1:H4,4,FALSE)				
C	**D**	**E**	**F**	**G**	**H**
Order ID	101011	101012	101013	101014	101015
Customer name	Jake	Wojciech	Frida	Sean	Tomisin
Product	Notepad	Pencils	Pens	Calculator	Highlighters
Price Paid	£5.00	£3.00	£6.00	£20.00	£8.00
Order ID Search	**Price Paid**				
101013	£6.00				

- The '**lookup_value**' has been typed in under the 'Order ID Search' heading (this forms the basis of the search and must relate to a value contained within the *first* row of cells). Cells D1 to H4 have been selected as the '**table_array**'. 4 has been selected as the '**row_index_number**' as we want to ascertain the price paid and this data is in the fourth row from the top. 'FALSE' has been entered into the '**range_lookup**' section of the formula, as we only want to return data that corresponds to the specified '**lookup_value**' (i.e. order number 101013).

Note that the **VLOOKUP** and **HLOOKUP** functions have some limitations. For instance, with **VLOOKUP**, your lookup column must be in the leftmost column of the selected group of cells. Limitations such as these can be overcome by combining the **INDEX** and **MATCH** functions, which can provide a more efficient and flexible tool. Once you are familiar with (the simpler) **VLOOKUP**, it may be worth reading up on the **INDEX MATCH** function.

City Career Series

General Interview & Internship Preparation

Writing Applications & Preparing For Interviews

This handbook focuses primarily on the commercial knowledge required for commercial awareness and case study interviews. This section provides only a brief overview of the other elements that are most commonly found in interviews in order to provide you with some insight into the other preparation you should undertake before attending an interview. For in depth coverage of these elements, read the City Career Series: Application, Interview & Internship Handbook (more information on this is given on the inside front cover of this handbook).

The recruitment process for City careers can involve an application stage, psychometric testing, a phone or Skype/video interview and an assessment centre at the firm's offices. These stages are designed to test your strengths, capabilities and suitability to the role for which you are applying. Other than the technical element already addressed previously in this handbook, there are four other key elements that firms tend to focus on when setting application questions and interviewing candidates. These are:

1. Competencies, Strengths & Experience

2. Career Motivation

3. Firm Motivation & Research

4. Current Affairs & The Financial Services Industry (another element of "commercial awareness")

When preparing for interviews, I created separate documents for each of these elements and highlighted the documents on the morning of each interview, much like revising for an exam. All the elements tend to be relevant (at least to some extent) to most City interviews. Once you have covered these elements in detail, it should therefore take less time to prepare for subsequent interviews. However, ensure you tailor your preparation depending on the firm you are interviewing at (and the role you are applying for).

It is important that you never lie during interviews and that you are able to substantiate any statements you make. Recruiters are very skilled at noticing if you are trying to bluff your way through (you may be asked to provide a lot of detail when recounting experiences). Getting caught lying or overly-embellishing the truth reflects negatively upon your character and is likely to cause recruiters to question the other statements you have made. At the end of the day, they are looking to get to know *you*. Throughout interviews, firms will in addition look for composure, confidence, clear articulation, strong interpersonal skills and enthusiasm. Try to keep calm and do not be afraid to disagree with interviewers, so long as you can justify your comments and are sure you are not objectively wrong!

Competencies, Strengths & Experience

- Firms will want to gain an insight into the skills and capabilities you have developed through your studies and extra curricular activities. Remind yourself of your personal experiences, positions of responsibility and extracurricular involvement. Focus on the skills and abilities you developed.

- It is good to use a range of different examples in your applications and interviews, both academic and non-academic. This can help to demonstrate that you are a well-rounded individual. Try to demonstrate how your interests, experiences, competencies and strengths are relevant to the role for which you are applying and why they make you an ideal candidate. For instance, if you have worked in a supermarket, this could demonstrate work ethic, commitment and experience dealing with clients (clients are essentially customers), whilst evidencing that you have developed soft skills such as problem solving (if things have gone wrong) and negotiating.

- Helpful preparation can include listing out all the interesting and/or relevant experiences that you have accumulated. Include positions of responsibility you have held, societies and sports teams you have been involved with, interesting group projects you have undertaken at university, part-time jobs and work experience in industries relevant to the organisation to which you are applying. Consider the particular skills and strengths that could be drawn out of each. You should then be ready for competency-based questions.

We have supplemented this section with a series of videos and articles relating to answering competency and strengths-based questions. These can be found at:

www.CityCareerSeries.com → Applications & Interviews → Competencies

Career Motivation

- Firms will want to understand your motivation for pursuing your career of choice. Consider how your experiences have influenced your decision to pursue your desired career.

- Tell the story of how your interest in your chosen career has developed. For instance, when and why did your interest in your chosen career first materialise? Was it at school whilst studying a particular subject, whilst undertaking work experience, or following a conversation with an acquaintance working in that industry? What did you do to further explore this interest (e.g. undertake certain work experience)? How did your research confirm that this was the right career for you? Ensure your answer is sensible however. Stating that you have always wanted to be a banker may not come across as genuine and believable to your interviewer!

We have supplemented the above section with a series of videos and articles relating to career motivation questions. These can be found at:

www.CityCareerSeries.com → Applications & Interviews → Motivation Questions

Firm Motivation & Research

- Firms will want to know your reasons for wanting to work for them. Research the firm at which you are interviewing in depth so that you are able to differentiate it from its competitors and explain why these differentiating factors particularly appeal to you.

- Do not give generic reasons for applying to that firm that merely reflect a quick skim of the firm's marketing materials. Think of legitimate ways to differentiate the firm and more importantly, relate these elements back to you in order to convince recruiters that these factors genuinely appeal. Which of your personal experiences have made the firm's culture, values, reputation and training structure appeal to you?

- You can access information on firms through a number of sources. You could start with the firm's website, its annual review, articles it has published and its profile on other websites. Follow the firm on Twitter, LinkedIn and Facebook and keep up to date with firm news relating to deals, poignant developments, awards and expansion plans. Sources such as the Financial Times and the Economist can also be useful.

We have supplemented the above section with a series of videos and articles relating to firm motivation questions. These can be found at:

www.CityCareerSeries.com → Applications & Interviews → Motivation Questions

Current Affairs & The Financial Services Industry

- Firms may want to see evidence of your interest in and understanding of current affairs and the industry you are looking to work in. Build up your knowledge and understanding of current affairs to evidence your interest in the wider economy. Relate your knowledge to your prospective employer, its clients and the markets in which they operate. You should also research the challenges the industry is facing and assess proposed solutions.

- If there is a particular topic that is consistently discussed on the front pages prior to your interview (for instance, regulation, tax avoidance, political instability, elections, disasters, emerging markets, whether Scotland should become independent, whether England should remain in the EU etc.), then try to gain some insight into the topic before the interview. There is every chance the interviewer will bring it up.

- In addition, check the front page of the Financial Times on the morning of your interview just in case something major has happened. A topic that comes up fairly often in some way or another is the challenges facing the Financial Services industry. You may for instance be asked what challenges the firm is facing, or what you would do if you took over the firm today.

- There are many other sources you can use to build your awareness, knowledge and understanding of current affairs. BBC Business News (online) provides a concise and straightforward account of current affairs. Helpfully, there are usually links at the bottom of articles to related articles. Reading these can help you to build a more comprehensive understanding of different topics. The Financial Times and the Economist similarly provide an overview of the most relevant topical issues affecting the business and finance world. Some sources let you subscribe to useful 'daily digest' summaries of key news articles, which can really help to keep you abreast of what is going on in the business world. Consider following well-known commentators and publications on Twitter, delving into blogs focusing on financial services, reading client alerts published by firms and searching out YouTube videos focusing on particular topical issues.

We have produced a series of articles analysing a variety of different industries. These can be found at:

www.CityCareerSeries.com → Commercial Awareness → Industry Analyses

We have produced a series of articles explaining and analysing topical current affairs. Read these at:

www.CityCareerSeries.com → Commercial Awareness → Topical Current Affairs

We produce weekly topical news summaries, which can be viewed at:

www.CityCareerSeries.com → Commercial Awareness → Headlines

Subscribe to our mailing list to receive these news summaries by email. You can do this at:

www.CityCareerSeries.com → Connect → Sign Up

Converting Internships Into Full-time Jobs

Approaching The Work

- If you cannot do the work to the standard expected by the firm, they will be unlikely to offer you a job. Whilst some pieces of set work will be harder than others, and minor mistakes may be completely fine, general attention to detail should never be overlooked. Proof read your work multiple times (even ask colleagues to have a read if you think this might be appropriate) and make sure there are no spelling, grammatical or formatting errors. These can be easily avoided.

- Check to see whether there are particular fonts, templates or settings in Microsoft Word or Excel that firms use as part of their 'house style' and where possible, adhere to these. This demonstrates your ability to absorb (and work in a way that aligns with) the ways in which the firm operates, whilst also ensuring the people judging your work will approve of it stylistically. There may also be templates of spreadsheets and financial models that you can edit rather than having to start from scratch. Research and/or ask. You could also see whether the firm has an intranet and/or support departments that can help (e.g. Knowledge Management departments).

- Consider the intended recipient of the work. If it is for a client, then ensure it is short, concise and to the point (unless you are told otherwise) and that the language is not too technical or full of jargon and acronyms. If the work is for a senior employee, perhaps query whether they would like you to reference the work (this means indicating the sources from which you found the information included), whether they have a rough word limit in mind, whether they would like a printed and/or an electronic copy and perhaps even whether they would like single or double sided printing. These are not stupid questions and can help to ensure the work is perceived as favourably as possible.

- Whenever you meet with someone, bring a pad and pen so that you are ready to write down instructions if you are set a new piece of work. Once you have received the instructions, you could summarise them back to your supervisor to check that you have understood them correctly. Ask questions if you are unclear on a particular instruction, but listen carefully. Asking the same question twice will waste your supervisor's time and reflect negatively on you. Try to figure out as much as possible by yourself through researching carefully. You could try to list out questions that arise as you run into difficulties and then ask them all at once when your supervisor has a free moment. Repeatedly interrupting your supervisor every time you have a question could frustrate him or her and disrupt his or her own work.

- Keep a work diary as you go along. You will then be able to reflect back on your previous work if questioned by your supervisor or an interviewer at a later stage. However, do not forget about confidentiality. If you include confidential information in your work diary, then consider refraining from taking it outside the office (during or after your internship). You could alternatively include just enough information to jog your memory about what you were doing, without including confidential client information. When making a job application after completing an internship, never include confidential details of work completed elsewhere. This could call into question your ability to adhere to the required standards of confidentiality.

Professionalism

- Be open and approachable. Try to meet as many people as you can. This could mean asking to sit in another division for a few hours or simply going for coffees with members of your team.

- Be professional and reliable. It should go without saying, but be punctual (especially following a social event that ended late). Do not be too informal, as this could be mistaken for arrogance. Check what the dress code is before you arrive and remain smart and presentable (even if some of the employees take a more casual approach). This does not necessarily mean you must ignore casual Fridays for instance, but do not show up in shorts and flip-flops simply because you have seen a Partner or Director do so.

- Remember you are making an impression on the entire firm. Treat everyone with courtesy and respect, whether they are your supervisor, the receptionists, the most senior employees at the firm, the secretaries or the cleaners. You are being assessed at all times and you never know who graduate recruitment will approach for an opinion on you throughout/after the internship.

- I have heard stories of interns talking negatively about other interns, not realising that one of the group to which they were speaking happened to be a good friend of that intern from university. Graduate recruiters can typically perceive any animosity caused in such a manner, which in my personal experience has not done any favours for those speaking negatively of others. Your fellow interns may well be your future colleagues so treat them well in order to ensure that a positive working relationship ensues in the future.

- I have heard candidates at times talk negatively about other firms to graduate recruitment representatives, presumably intending to demonstrate that the current firm is their preference. This could be a huge mistake. Firstly, bad mouthing other firms could convey a degree of arrogance and suggest that you lack professionalism. Secondly, graduate recruiters tend to move between firms fairly regularly and may well end up at the firm that you were badmouthing before that firm has made their final decision about whether to offer you a job. Two of the graduate recruiters running the final internship that I undertook had worked at other firms at the same time that I had attended open days and internships at those other firms. One had even looked after me on my interview day at a different firm only 5 months earlier! Moral of the story? Be careful what you say to your colleagues and to graduate recruiters. Remain professional and do not talk negatively about other people and firms - it does not reflect well on you!

Group Work & Team Presentations

- Many City careers involve employees having to regularly work in teams. This may be internally within their particular departments; internally within their firm but with a number of different departments that have a role on a different aspect of a deal (for instance the tax or regulatory implications of a transaction); with employees working within a different office within the global network of offices (if the firm is international); and/or with other types of firms. For instance, many transactions involve input from investment banks, commercial law firms, accountancy firms, consultancy firms, regulators and institutional investors and these different industry players must coordinate effectively in order to successfully execute the transaction at hand.

- Internships (and some assessment days) typically include a team-based exercise to test the way in which candidates interact with others on a mutual task. This could involve completing a creative task in a group, for instance building a Lego tower in line with specific instructions. It could involve researching and delivering a group presentation relating to the firm in general or a particular department. This may be structured as a pitch to a fictional client that focuses on the firm's capabilities, its past experience, the challenges it is facing, the locations in which new offices should be opened, or even the way in which it can offer value for money to clients (perhaps addressing fee structures or value-adding services). Alternatively, group exercises could involve engaging in fictitious commercial negotiations (sometimes with more than 2 opposing sides) or discussing various investment options as a group before agreeing which one to pursue. These exercises may also be designed to test candidates' commercial awareness and knowledge of the firm.

- Graduate recruiters are very perceptive and are likely to notice if the attitude of one or two candidates adversely impacts upon the team dynamic (even if this dynamic only surfaces when candidates are working together in private). Try to work well with team members. Encourage quieter team members to speak, be receptive of ideas (or constructively contribute to ideas you believe are less strong). You could try to link ideas together and draw on others' contributions, arrive at meetings on time and having completed your delegated work and above all, avoid being rude, overbearing or competitive. Candidates who are outwardly competitive are not generally looked upon favourably. Such an attitude can indicate that candidates will negatively impact upon the firm's culture if they were to be offered a job. After all, these exercises are about collaboration, not competition!

- Many presentations are followed by question and answer sessions. If you have worked on a presentation in a team, then make sure you know each other's work and research inside out. You may be allowed to defer an answer to a colleague, but equally you may be expected to answer questions on your colleagues' work. If you are clearly familiar with each other's input then this provides an indication to your assessors that you have worked effectively as a team. You may also want to consider supplementing a presentation with a handout. This can enhance your presentation and make your group stand out, whilst also demonstrating creativity, effective teamwork and strong organisation. However, perhaps consider giving out the handout after your speech as it may otherwise distract those in the room from what you have to say.

- Many graduate recruiters claim that there are enough jobs available for a majority of internship candidates if they are all good enough at the work and a strong enough fit for the firm. Acting competitively during group exercises is more likely to lose you an offer than help you to secure one! Barclays have provided some further advice relating to group exercises on the next page.

Demonstrating Your Motivation

-   You are selling yourself during an internship as much as a firm is selling itself to you. Your personality will therefore influence a firm's inclination (or not!) to hire you. They will look for genuine commitment to your chosen career, as they would rather not invest in you, only for you to leave a short way into your career. They will look to see how well you fit in with the firm's culture. Do you get on well with the firm's existing employees? They will look to see whether you are a hard worker. Have you asked around for work if your supervisor has nothing for you, or have you avoided responsibility or failed to show a genuine interest in the work?

-   Your behaviour will influence whether a firm believes you have the ability to complete work in a very demanding, client-led environment and whether you can be trusted to work with high-profile clients and professional services firms that expect only the very best from their advisors and colleagues. Some roles may also require ample confidence and presentation skills. If this is the case, think about whether you are the quiet person in the corner, or the person making an effort to get involved and socialise and how this could in turn reflect on your ability to fulfil the role for which you are applying.

-   If you have not received enough work, then request more (you could offer other departments a hand if appropriate). Remember, everything is a learning opportunity, so do not complain if you are set boring or repetitive tasks. You will inevitably receive such tasks at the start of your career if you end up working for the firm in the future. Avoid looking as if you would not be prepared to pitch in and get things done.

Enthusiasm

-   One of the pieces of feedback that many rejected candidates receive after an internship is that their enthusiasm for the firm was lacking. It is easy to assume that if you are clever enough to do the work that the role will require you to do, then surely this should be enough. However, if you do not seem enthusiastic when spending only a few weeks (or months) at the firm, this could give the impression that 6 months or a year down the line, perhaps you will no longer care at all. This could in turn affect the quality of your work, impact negatively upon the teams you work in and adversely affect the culture of the firm.

-   Firms will be less willing to hire someone who may potentially negatively impact the firm's culture. Firms generally perceive their culture as something that keeps employees motivated (and thus from a commercial standpoint, boosts productivity). It's not difficult to smile for a few weeks!

-   In addition (although this is merely an opinion and is not necessarily reflective of the way all firms operate), firms may be less willing to make offers if they do not believe candidates will accept. This is partially due to the fact that it will be harder to recruit the required number of people (e.g. schedule the right number of interviews or make the right number of offers) if the firm has no idea how many candidates are likely to accept their offers. A lack of enthusiasm may indicate a candidate will quit after only a short period at the firm, meaning that the money invested in training them throughout an internship and the early stages of their career will be wasted.

-   You can demonstrate enthusiasm simply by getting involved in as much as you can. Ask lots of carefully considered questions (to your supervisors, graduate recruitment, people you meet during socials and people that give you presentations). Asking questions can really help to demonstrate your genuine interest in the firm.

-   Attend as many social and networking events as possible (although of course do not let this affect the quality of your work if you are facing tight deadlines and avoid drinking too much alcohol!). Attendance at these events can demonstrate your interest in integrating into the firm, getting to know your potential future colleagues (including other interns and existing employees) and contributing to the firm's culture. Repeatedly avoiding such events could indicate that you would perhaps rather be working elsewhere, or that you have little interest in familiarising yourself with the firm's employees or its culture. This in turn may also reflect negatively upon your interest in networking (a skill that is essential to facilitate effective team working, especially when external parties are involved) and your motivation for working at that particular firm.

-   However, if there are any cultural circumstances that impinge upon your ability to socialise to the same extent as others (for instance if, during Ramadan, you are due to open the fast at the same time that a social is taking place), then explain the situation to the graduate recruitment team.

Final / Fast-track Interviews

-   Whilst three or four structured reasons for wanting to work at a particular firm may scrape you through an interview to secure an internship, much more may be expected of you in an end-of-internship interview. Having spent a number of weeks immersed in a firm's culture, meeting many employees and engaging in real work, your reasons for wanting to work at the firm will have to be more personal, more substantive and less derisive of graduate recruitment marketing materials.

-   For instance, was there a similar type of personality within the firm? People you particularly enjoyed meeting? A culture that really resonated with you (if so, describe this culture and why it appeals)? Pieces of work that were particularly interesting and indicative of the type of work that the firm carries out? Did you attend a presentation on the structure of the training that helped to differentiate the firm from its competitors or align the firm with your preferred means of learning and developing?

-   Be ready to discuss the work you have completed in detail and perhaps how this work fits in with the wider context of the firm's operations. Prepare some carefully considered questions for your interviewers. These could perhaps relate to the firm's culture, its future strategies, the challenges it is facing (or may face in the future), its training or anything else you can think of that demonstrates your genuine interest in working there. If you do ask about the firm's challenges and future strategies however, make sure you have undertaken some related research as you may be asked to express a personal opinion.

-   Be prepared to give feedback. What have you enjoyed? What did you not enjoy? How does the firm compare to other firms you have interned at? Has your opinion of the firm changed since your internship commenced? If so, how? What has differed from your expectations and preconceptions?

We have supplemented this section with a series of videos relating to converting internships into full-time jobs. These can be found at:

www.CityCareerSeries.com → Internships → Converting Internships

Further Reading

Christopher Stoakes was the author that inspired Jake Schogger to set up City Career Series and write this handbook with colleagues. As a former financial journalist, City lawyer, management consultant and top trainer, he knows the business and financial worlds inside out. His engaging style and ability to explain complex concepts with surprising simplicity meant that his books played a significant role in helping most of this handbook's authors prepare for their interviews. As such, the authors strongly recommend that you supplement your study of this handbook by reading some (or all) of the books detailed below.

Understand the financial markets

Anyone who works in business these days needs to understand the financial world. All You Need To Know About The City is the best-selling guide that students and young professionals use to get up-to-speed quickly and painlessly. It uses the simple analogy of a market to explain who the participants are (issuers, intermediaries and institutional investors). It looks at what they buy and sell, from shares and bonds to foreign exchange, derivatives and securitisations. It examines the lifecycle of a company and the anatomy of a global bank. It explains why interest rates change and how they drive markets. In short, it enables you to understand the financial markets with no prior knowledge.

Enhance your commercial awareness

If you want a job in the business world you need to be commercially aware. What is it and how do you get it? All You Need To Know About Commercial Awareness tells you. It explains what matters to businesses, how they are funded, the importance of cash flow, the purpose of strategy and the quest for customers. It explains how companies are organised and what they are looking for when you apply for a job. This book contextualises much of the information within this handbook, providing an excellent supplementary read.

Write well at work

A majority of firms require candidates to submit written assignments as part of the interview and/or internship assessment process. Candidates are expected to write concisely and accurately and frame their words within a clear and coherent structure. However, employers complain that young people can't write. What are they looking for and how can you deliver it? Get To The Point explains how. Writing well in the workplace is critical to your career. Words are still the principal form of communication between people in business. Write well and you will shine. Write badly and you could torpedo your career.

We have produced some additional resources to help you build your commercial awareness. These can be found at:

www.CityCareerSeries.com → **Commercial Awareness** → **Developing Your Commercial Awareness**